"Lisa Bloom offers asp ... an innovative approacl ... of some of our best wis ... ... worth reading, but Bloom adds her ow ... coaching success. Good advice designed to be there when you need it."

Annette Simmons
Author of 'The Story Factor' and 'Whoever Tells the Best Story Wins'

"Lisa Bloom's book, *Cinderella and the Coach – The Power of Story-telling for Coaching Success*, is a 'must read' for every coach who wants to get life changing, lasting results with clients. Everything you need know to achieve a successful, thriving coaching business and a life of freedom and fulfillment you will find in these masterfully written pages."

Viki Winterton, Coach and Change Agent to Fortune 100 Companies, Founder Expert Insights Family of Opportunity www.getei.com

"I was already in a BIG believer in the power of stories and the impact it can have on building a business and anchoring learning. After reading this book, Lisa just took my belief to a whole new stratosphere. I was on the edge of my seat. Who knew learning could be so much fun?! I LOVE this book...it's not just for coaches. It's for anyone who is in business."

Jeanna Gabellini
MasterPeaceCoaching.com

Lisa Bloom's new book is a powerful and absorbing read that is a must for any new coach just getting started, or any existing coach who is ready to take their business to the next level by adding advanced coaching techniques. Lisa is a brilliant writer with a witty and engaging sense of humor that will keep you entertained while you also learn some incredible groundbreaking, results-driven information for a successful, thriving coaching practice. Get it today and get ready for the story of your success!

Dawn Caryl Allen, CDC dawncarylallen.com

"People love stories. People remember stories. And people are inspired by stories. That's why storytelling is one of the most powerful skills you can develop to enhance the depth of your coaching and the effectiveness of your marketing. Lisa Bloom's engaging new book, "Cinderella and the Coach" is a wonderful read and helpful handbook for coaches who want to incorporate the powerful art of storytelling into their coaching. A must-read for every coach who wants to bring more creativity to their business!"

Michelle Schubnel
President & Head Coach
www.CoachAndGrowRich.com

Cinderella and the Coach—

the Power of Storytelling for Coaching Success!

Lisa Bloom

Copyright © 2011 Lisa Bloom
All rights reserved.

ISBN: 1463782101
ISBN-13: 9781463782108

Dedication

* * *

To my parents for the best start ever, knowing I could dream it and make it happen!   And to Ilan and the boys — my best support, my best audience and my best critics.

Thank you with all my heart!

Acknowledgement

* * *

Thanks to Niall MacMonagle for seeing in me what I could not yet see in myself, to Brendan Kennelly who told me "there's a book in you— get it out!" To Robyn, Karen and Bill of the ICA who saw my vision. To Dawn for keeping me on track.

Thanks to my amazing clients who continue to inspire me to find my stories.

About the author

* * *

There was once a girl who grew up in a traditional home in Ireland. Surrounded by the beautiful countryside (it really is greener than anywhere else!), amazing stories of pixies and leprechauns, and the warmth of Jewish practice; she grew up to love to hear and tell stories!

Lisa has travelled widely and taken on many jobs; Stable-girl, galley-slave, bar-tender, photographer, rape crisis counselor, mother, entrepreneur, writer, coach, trainer and storyteller.

She is convinced that telling a good story is the remedy for most ills!

Lisa has a BA from Tel Aviv University and an MBA from Boston University.

She is the founder of Story Coach Inc. http://www.story-coach.com, developing creative solutions for coaches, trainers and entrepreneurs to beat overwhelm and stress and discomfort with marketing to find confidence, attract ideal clients and make more money by finding their success story.

Lisa's 'Certified Story Coach™ Program' is accredited by the International Coach Federation and is one of a kind, worldwide.

She lives in Israel with her partner and their 4 boys!

Table of Contents

* * *

Story Index

* * *

Introduction

* * *

**"Tell me a fact, and I may learn something.
Tell me a truth, and I might believe.
Tell me a theory and I'll see if it works.
Tell me a story, and it may live in my heart forever."**

–Indian Proverb

The Golden Key

In the winter time, when deep snow lay on the ground, a poor boy was forced to go out on a sledge to fetch wood. When he had gathered it together, and packed it, he wished, as he was so frozen with cold, not to go home at once, but to light a fire and warm himself a little. So he scraped away the snow and as he was thus clearing the ground, he found a tiny golden key. Hereupon he thought that where the key was, the lock must be also, and dug in the ground and found an iron chest. "If the key does but fit it?" thought he; "no doubt there are precious things in that little box". He searched, but no keyhole was there. At last he discovered one, but so small that it was hardly visible. He tried it, and the key fitted it exactly. Then he turned it once round and now we must wait until he has quite unlocked it and opened the lid, and then we shall learn what wonderful things were lying in that box.

Grimm's Brothers

I magine that this book is the magic box. I am delighted to invite you to take hold of the golden key and turn the lock gently but firmly. I can tell you that the treasures held within are but the stories of hearts and minds, and my greatest wish is that you recognize yours here too! The ideal place to open up the magic box is in the company of dear friends, good people, around an open fire; the people in your life with whom you can share a good story.

Once upon a time, in the olden days, as my mother would say, if you had a problem, you were expected to just put your head down, ignore it, work through it or somehow just get by. The only people who 'got help' were the crazy ones and it wasn't the kind of help that 'normal' people needed. There were no books to read, no websites or resources to research to help you cope with your difficulties. There were no coaches.

Nowadays, getting help has become so much easier. It's perfectly acceptable to go for therapy, to go on a retreat or learn meditation. There are many alternative treatments and the coaching industry is thriving. Finally, people are recognizing that coaching is not just for sporting excellence, but that help is at hand for people who are struggling with life issues. And it's not just for when you are struggling; this generation has an expectation to thrive. But how do we thrive? Well, get a coach. They seem to know some secrets that will help.

Coaching schools are doing really well. Bright eyed and bushy tailed coaches are hitting the market, ready to change the world, ready to help people reach their potential and learn to excel in every part of their life.

Sounds great, right?

And it would be, if it were true.

You see, a lot of coaches are leaving coaching school, or even life's school, with some great skills, often a wonderful vision, and sometimes great tools. They have passion and drive. They honestly want to help people and make the world a better and happier place.

And this is just about when the problems start.

Unfortunately, when you look at the statistics, you'll see that only one in five coaches actually makes a living, and that the majority of coaches who would love to spend all their time coaching, actually can't afford to. The earnings of the average coach are not exactly attractive. Yet research shows that over 80% of those people who have experienced coaching have been 'very satisfied'. And that the return of investment for companies that implement Executive Coaching more than proves itself.

So, there's something missing here. Something doesn't make sense.

Nowadays, potential clients don't know who to pick to help them find their way. They are inundated by all kinds of people, including internet marketers telling them the quick and easy way to get rich, happy, thin, fit, smart, educated, and sexy, and anything else you can think of!

So, if you're a coach, you need to do some really important things in order to be heard above this noise. You need to provide a trust-based relationship with your potential client, you need to differentiate yourself from others in the market; you need to be super-confident about your skills and you need to be crystal clear about what you are offering.

And yes, you guessed it – that's exactly what Story Coaching can offer you.

This is not a nice-to-have little system. This is a revolutionary approach to the coaching industry. But I'll come back to that later... first let me tell you my story.

I had just finished my training as a Professional Coach and set up shop. I was delighted with the new direction in my career having spent years in corporate training and development. My friend and I were sitting in a café and I was telling her all about my new profession, how powerful coaching was and how much I loved it. And then she said something...and everything changed.

"So Lisa, what would make me hire you rather than any of the other well-known coaches who have a PhD. and an established company behind them?" I started stammering, "Well, uh... it's just that...." The truth is I had no idea how to answer that question. And it stayed with me for a very long time.

Let me tell you more.

I have been telling stories my whole life. When I started studying to be a Professional Storyteller, anyone who knew me well, admitted that this was what I was born to do. When I got up on the stage for the very first time as a Storyteller, I felt at home. When I tell stories,

I come alive – I am connected to the storytellers that came before me and those that will come after. I am blessed to be a keeper of the sacred fire.

As I pondered the question, "Why would anyone hire me?" I knew it was connected to my storytelling, but it took me a long time to figure out how and why. And then one day it all came together. I realized that we are all storytellers and the stories that we tell determine our reality.

I started asking, "What happens when we really look at these stories?", "What happens when we question them and when we inquire into how our stories serve us?"

Eureka! That's that storytelling coaching connection.

So here's the bottom line – I found my story. I found the story of my life and my business and as a result, I have had phenomenal results.

It has differentiated me from other coaches. It has given me the marketing edge. I have a successful coaching business, I have speaking engagements and clients all over the world. And my clients are finding their niche and attracting clients as a result of having discovered and inquired into their stories.

Using Story Coaching enables coaches to quickly and easily transform their lives and businesses, and those of their clients…it's as simple and powerful as that!

Story Coaching is a proven way to develop coaching expertise as it is modeled on core coaching competencies. Get them and you get to coach at a much higher level, guaranteed! It ensures that you attract more of your ideal clients while differentiating yourself from other coaches.

Story Coaching, is all about how to use stories and storytelling (in many different ways) to be a more effective coach, to take the stress out of marketing to attract more clients. In fact, it is the easiest and most effective way to attract ideal, high-paying clients.

And this last point is really important, it is not only possible but easy to do this; and not just for those born storytellers, it's possible for everyone. We ARE all storytellers. It's time to start using stories more effectively and more powerfully in our lives and in our businesses.

This book is all about how to do just that.

You'll learn how to be an inspiring, compelling and expert Story Coach – attract amazing clients and having them running back for more!

You'll learn how storytelling is an integral part of every aspect of coaching.

You'll learn how to apply Story Coaching concepts to every core coaching competency and become an even better coach!

Welcome to 'Cinderella & the Coach – the Power of Storytelling for Coaching Success!'

CHAPTER 1 –

In the beginning was the word....and then there were stories!

$$* * *$$

"there's treasure to be discovered, and it's inside you.... story is a force so powerful and enduring that it has shaped cultures, religions, whole civilizations."

-Peter Guber, "Tell to Win"

Truth & the Story

Long, long ago there was a woman who travelled the world. She travelled so far and for so long that she grew old and tired. And she decided she needed to rest. When she arrived at the very next village, she walked through the gates of the village and went up to the first house. She knocked on the door and it opened just a tiny bit, and then slammed shut in her face. When she knocked on the door of the next house, the window on the first floor opened up a tiny crack, but then closed again. And at the third house there was no answer at all. And so she went around most of the village, but no one would open their door. Nobody would let her in. The old woman returned to the gates of the village and sat down and waited.

Sometime later, a young man arrived at the village. He was tall and very handsome. He had beautiful long hair and a cape that flowed behind him. The young man rode a handsome white horse and as he rode through the gates of the village, the doors opened and the people poured out of their houses to greet him.

They brought food and music. There was a great celebration in his honor. And the old woman sat at the gates and watched.

And when the commotion died down somewhat, the old woman went up to the young man and asked him, "Who are you? And how is it that the people here were so happy to see you and greeted you so warmly, whereas me they left outside?" The young man said, "I am the Story, who are you?" The old woman replied, "I am the Truth." She thought for a moment and then she said," Why don't you take me under your cape and then together we can enter every place." The young man agreed.

And so it is from that day until now, whenever you hear a story, you can be sure that somewhere, hidden well (or maybe not hidden at all) there will be at least a little bit of truth.

This story was told to me by Sharon Aviv, a wonderful Storyteller and Teacher

The Story Coaching Opportunity

If you are a coach, or thinking about becoming a coach, there are a few things you need to know.

- **Coaching Skills**

You need to know what it takes to be a good coach

- **Business Knowledge**

You need to know what running a coaching business looks like.

- **Niche Discovery**

You need to figure out who you want to work with.

- **Client Attraction**

You need to figure out how to get clients.

If you've been doing this for a while, you may have clients already, probably not enough, and you may need to find a good business model that will leverage your time while bringing in continuous new prospects.

But here's the good news. The world has never been more ready for expert coaches. There has never before been such widespread awareness of the coaching industry. There has never been so much money spent on self-development and self-help books, products and services world-wide. It is our time. Now is the time to get out there and create the business and life-style that you dream of.

And focusing in on the power of Storytelling is the way to do it!

My Story

I was working as the Training and Development Manager for a Software Development Company. I was in the corporate classroom, teaching a class for mid-level Managers. I was not enormously inspired by the material that had been developed by the centralized corporate training staff. I started telling stories to illustrate the points I needed to make. At first, it was just whatever came to my head, but then something really magical happened. I noticed that every time I told a story, the level of engagement in the room sky-rocketed. Every time I would start an anecdote or narrative about something 'real', my audience was super-engaged. I realized I was on to something. When I used stories, I reached my audience in an entirely different way.

So, I started to plan for the stories, to work them into the curriculum, to do it on purpose, and stop making them up on the spot! The results were very clear. Not only were my program attendees more engaged, they were more excited about learning, retained the information better and created stronger relationships within the experience, both with me and their co-trainees. I was meeting my targets better. It was totally win-win.

I had simply become aware of the power of story in the business context. I noticed that the best leaders were great storytellers. By telling stories these phenomenal leaders inspired their teams and companies and created massive buy-in for all kinds of strategic and change initiatives.

Once I left the corporate arena, I began to notice how story and storytelling is relevant in many fields. As I started focusing on Coaching, I saw that Storytelling is an incredibly powerful way to coach and to create a coaching business.

The Coaching Industry

There are some really wonderful coaches out there, doing great work in the world. As a former cynic and critic of the industry, I have been completely converted. This is purely as a result of my personal experience of coaching. When I work with a coach, I am productive, positive, intuitive, confident, and get great results. There is no doubt that coaching simply works.

However, there are several challenges for coaches.

Firstly, a lot of coaches get stuck in the process and don't feel that they can bring their own specific creativity and personality into their coaching model, and subsequent success.

Secondly, with the great financial challenges that people face nowadays, coaches don't know how to market their value.

Thirdly, people no longer know who they can trust and this is reflected in their consumer decisions. As a business person, you need to generate trust immediately or you will have difficulty getting anyone to invest in you.

A new approach is needed for the business and practice of Coaching; an approach that will cater to all of these significant challenges.

If you can understand what great gifts you bring to your practice and the story of who you are in your coaching, you can create a successful business.

If you can talk about the benefits of what you do, if you can tell the story of the transformation that you offer your clients, you can create a successful business.

If you can instill trust (your story is the best way to do this), you can give people the experience of your authenticity in how you show up in your coaching then you too can create a successful business.

Let me tell you a story!

After almost six months without contact, I gave a courtesy call to a client, the representative of a wonderful organization, that I'd really enjoyed working with in the past.

"Are you in the car behind me?" she asked.

"No," I laughed, "Should I be?"

She continued, "You see, I've just turned off the highway into your town. I thought maybe you saw me in the car?"

"No, I was just thinking about you. Wondering what you guys are up to and how everything is?" I replied. "I'm in my office!"

"How strange," she said. "Will you come and meet us for coffee? We're getting together," she added referring to her colleague. "We'd both love to see you and have some ideas and plans to discuss with you!"

"I'd love to," I said.

As I drove up to the coffee shop where they were meeting, I was smiling to myself thinking about how the universe delivers every single time.

I realized that it was exactly a year since my first meeting with these wonderful women.

It was the same kind of day, with a warm breeze, the feeling that spring was here and summer not far away.

The purple blossoms on the big tree at the edge of my neighborhood had just taken me by surprise.

Every year it seemed to appear overnight and then there were the magical two weeks where every day you thought it couldn't possibly get more beautiful, and yet it did!

Exactly a year ago, I had responded to a query on a local forum. They were looking for some support with public speaking skills and it was a non-profit organization whose ideology I love!

They asked to meet with me immediately.

The meeting happened the very next day.

I had done no preparation whatsoever. I met with them and simply told them my story; the story of who I am, what I do and how I could help their organization. And of course why I wanted to!

I was not at all nervous. I was not even slightly stressed. I just told my story.

And they loved it. Two days later, when a presenter dropped out of an important meeting they were holding, guess who they called? Yes, and I jumped at the chance to work with them and that led to another 6 workshops.

Never underestimate the power of your story.

When you are ready to tell it at the drop of a hat, amazing opportunities arise.

I have seen this happen again and again. When you can easily and eloquently articulate what it is that you do, what your blessings are in the world and how you can serve others, the universe delivers the chances for you to do just that!

And you'll get paid well for it too!

Just as the blossoms on the trees sneak up on me every year, the opportunities to learn, grow, serve and contribute are there at exactly the right time, sometimes hiding, sometimes right in front of my eyes.

The trick is to pay attention, to notice the beauty, the opportunity and be ready to take action and be truly grateful as it manifests.

Your story is the key to being ready to take action – so if you don't know how to tell it, now's the time to find out!

There has never been a better time for you to start realizing the power of your story!

Your Challenge!

Let's change the statistics for Coaching Business Success!

I'm tired of hearing how many coaches and entrepreneurs fail in the first few years of attempting to start a business.

Let's start learning how to tell the story of success as we create it!

Chapter 2 –

The Storytelling/ Coaching Connection

* * *

"It's all a question of story. We are in trouble just now because we do not have a good story. We are in between stories. The old story, the account of how the world came to be and how we fit into it, is no longer effective. Yet we have not learned the new story."

— *Thomas Berry, Theologian, Philosopher, and Cultural Historian*

The Rabbi & The Bird

There was once a wise Rabbi who always seemed to have the answer to every question, every problem. Often the answer was simply another question. He always knew what to say.

Now this Rabbi had many students and one day two of his students were talking about how annoying it was that the Rabbi always had all the answers! They thought it would be great to find a way that the Rabbi could be wrong.

The very next day, one of the students came up with a great idea. He held out his hands and said to his friend "Look here, I've caught a tiny bird and I'm holding it in my hands. Let's go and ask the great Rabbi a simple question that he can't possibly get right. We'll ask him if the bird is alive or dead! If the Rabbi answers that the bird is alive, I'll simply squeeze my hands tight and prove him wrong. If he says that the bird is dead, then I'll open my hands and let him fly away."

"This time we'll prove the great Rabbi wrong!"

So, that very day, they went up to the Rabbi in front of all the other students. With his hands held out in front of him the student said, "Great Rabbi, I have a question for you. I have a bird in my hands, is he alive or dead?"

The Rabbi thought for a moment, rubbed his chin and said, "The answer to this, my dear boy, is in your hands!"

Source Unknown

It IS all a question of story! And it is in your hands!

When we apply storytelling to coaching we get to Coach better, build a more authentic and powerful business, create success and live a life more fulfilled and joyful. It's all about the story!

What is Storytelling?

In the olden days, we sat around the fire and told stories. As the darkness fell and the night drew in, we told about the day that had passed, the people we had seen, the words that had been spoken, and the places we had visited. We told about other days, people and places. We understood the world and our place in it, through our stories. And then we told about our dreams and our memories, our passions and desires. We came alive through our stories! Storytelling is an age-old tradition originating in all cultures and in many different settings. It took place around the fire or over the washing of clothes in the river, or by the well while watering the animals. It took place at the market.

Nowadays, storytelling takes place on the bus, train, on the telephone, by email and during dinner parties. It is the way people have connected and shared their lives with each other since the beginning of time.

Throughout the generations, communities have passed down their stories from parent to child, preserving their history and culture, recording their experience, illustrating their values, creating continuity. We live in a world where there is a huge reliance on technology and where there is a vast amount of knowledge on every subject readily available to huge populations of people. In spite of this, or perhaps as a result of this, Storytelling as an art form is in the midst of a revival world-wide. People are craving the simplicity of traditional storytelling.

"Information simply leaves us feeling incompetent and lost. We don't need more information. We need to know what it means. We need a story that explains what it means and makes us feel like we fit in there somewhere."
- Annette Simmons, Author of "The Story Factor," 2006.

Storytelling is the oldest and most powerful tool of influence. It has become a critical skill to identify and develop in individuals and organizations for so many reasons; to communicate, to sell, to motivate and to inspire, to name just a few!

What is Story Coaching – the Storytelling & Coaching connection?

Story Coaching is a unique approach and methodology for the theory and practice of Coaching. It is based on understanding the power of storytelling to create awareness, broaden perspectives, increase learning and motivate action.

The concept is based on this simple premise.

As we experience life, we 'tell' it – almost every event that happens to us, we pass on as an anecdote or complaint, or amusing table-side story, or told purposefully and with interpretation. This is a completely subjective activity; we choose the words, the style, the characters and the plot of these stories. And in the 'telling', in the narrative we choose, we define our reality.

If we dare to look closely at the narrative, we can examine the stories we choose to tell. Some of the stories we tell serve us well, others do us a great disservice. Either way, as we inquire into them, we begin to understand how committed we have become to these stories. We are often fiercely committed to the very stories that keep us stuck, sabotage our goals and cripple us into complacency.

The stories that we tell help us identify our own strengths and areas for growth and learning. As we start to understand the power of the stories we tell, we can also start creating new stories. And the new stories can be better, much better. So that in choosing our own narrative in a mindful and positive way, we can create a better life. This is not about reinventing or rewriting history. It's about choosing to tell our stories in a more empowering way. It's about finding the perspective on our stories that serves us best.

Story Coaching is a creative and innovative approach that allows us to work with all the different types of storytelling in our Coaching Practice. It is a winning combination that is very powerful in business and personal life to motivate, inspire and achieve outstanding results.

TRY THIS!

(Exercise)

Think of the first storyteller in your life.
It may be a mother, father, grandparent, priest, rabbi, teacher or friend.
What do you remember? Where were you? How did you feel?
What effect did the storyteller and the stories have on you?
How does it feel to remember this experience?

As an adult, when we hear stories, from the very start of "Once upon a time…," we are brought back to that place and space in our childhood when our first storyteller told us stories. Usually this is a very special place associated with warmth, protection, nurturing, safety and love.

Every time you tell a story (especially a tradition tale), you are evoking this experience. It's a powerful place to work from!

Excerpt from a Story Coach's Journal!

I stood on the street corner and tried to summon up the courage to speak to her.

She was a rough spoken, rough looking woman. She had lines on her face that showed the hard life she was living. She had calloused hands and wide hips and her hair was tied up and sticking out under a woolen hat. Her mismatching woolen sweater looked handmade and worn. It was dirty and frayed at the edges. She had brown cigarette stains on her fingers accompanying her deep, loose cough.

And she had bright shining eyes and an expression that could easily break into a broad smile or transform into a frown and a yell.

She was selling flowers.

I was just 16 years old. I was involved in a school project to make a radio program on "Language - the good, the bad and the beautiful!"

The street seller had little time for me to interview her. Her eyes were darting to every passerby as she yelled to sell her wares at them.

Her language was colorful! Every sentence an array of images, every image held a story.

This woman with little or no education was an amazing storyteller. The stories she told described her life, both through what was said and what was not.

We spoke to bikers and business men. We spoke to shop-keepers, postmen and professors. And after all these years, a few gems have stayed with me.

Someone said, "There is no bad language, only bad minds and bad hearts..." This was amazing to me coming from a home where we were certainly not allowed use 'bad language'. I loved swear words, for the rough sounds and colorful shapes and of course because they were not allowed.

Now I know that bad language can only be in the untruth and pain of confusion and blame that turns into hurtful and destructive words.

And someone else reminded me of the scripture that says…in the beginning was the word…

And now I know that after the word, there came the story.

Since the beginning of language, since the beginning of time, we have told stories. The story is the truth, in the minds and hearts of the teller. And that is what matters.

Stories can be good, bad and beautiful. Stories are what we do, where we go, who we are; whether we realize it or not.

Stories are the way that we most often, most truthfully and most urgently show up in the world.

Are you telling the story that serves you best?

Well, next time you find yourself in the middle of a story, make it a good one!

CHAPTER 3 –

Can I tell you a Story? Establishing the Coaching Agreement

* * *

"Great stories agree with our worldview. The best stories don't teach people anything new. Instead, the best stories agree with what the audience already believes, and makes the members of the audience feel smart and secure when reminded how right they were in the first place."

— *Seth Godin, Author of "Tribes: We Need You to Lead Us"*

The Tale-Teller

Long, long ago, in the time of lords and ladies, castles and kings, monsters and dragons and magical rings, there was one who told, to young and old, tales of all these things.

The tale-teller traveled from village to village with his leather satchel over his shoulder, telling tales in exchange for a hot meal and a place to sleep ... and perhaps a new tale or two with him when he left. For tales are meant to be shared. If they're not told, they crumble into dust.

On the night my story takes place, the townspeople were rejoicing with the news that the tale-teller was coming. The lord of the manor had opened the Great Hall and declared a feast day, and all the people from miles around came to eat and drink and listen.

Among the listeners was a young maiden, a peasant girl, who was collecting food in her apron for her sister lying sick in bed at home. They lived alone, their parents having died.

When the tale-teller entered the hall, the people cheered. "Tell us a story! Tell us a story!"

The old man smiled and set his leather satchel down on a table. He opened it, and those who were nearest could see it was filled to the brim with polished stones.

"I've prepared a new one for you," he said, and picked up a stone from the top. Grasping it in his right hand, he pressed it against his heart, closed his eyes and took a long, slow breath. He opened his eyes.

"Once upon a time there dwelt a father and three sons ...," he began. His hand never left his heart.

The listeners leaned forward, hardly breathing, not wanting to miss a word. It was a story of a thrilling adventure, and when the tale-teller finished, the listeners cheered. The tale-teller took the stone away from his heart and replaced it in the satchel.

"Another! Another!" the people shouted, "A funny one!"

"Here's one you'll like," said the tale-teller, choosing a small red stone from the satchel. He placed it over his heart as before.

"One day in the forest a fox met a bear ..."

Soon the listeners were weak with laughter. When the tale-teller finished, they shouted, "Another! Another!"

"Do you have a love story?" asked a young couple nearby. The tale-teller smiled and said, "Of course." He reached into the satchel and pulled out a silver stone shaped like a teardrop.

"A long time ago there lived three sisters ..."

As he told this tale, tears formed in the eyes of his listeners, for the lovers had to undergo many trials to test their love. But there was one listener whose eyes were not wet.

This man was a thief, and he had come to the feast for the free food, not the stories. But when he saw the silver stone, his interest in this tale-teller grew.

Easily, like a snake, he slithered through the crowd until he stood beside the table where the satchel lay. His practiced eyes scanned the stones within.

These were no ordinary stones!

He would have to have a jeweler appraise them, of course, but he'd be willing to wager that he was looking at carnelians, opals, jade, amber, lapis lazuli and other semi-precious stones.

He hadn't even noticed that the tale-teller had finished his tale. The old man set the teardrop-shaped stone in the satchel right before the thief's eyes.

It was solid silver!

A stone like that would bring a good price, thought the thief, and waited for his chance. Suddenly it came.

"My friends, I must go refresh my thirst ... but I will return shortly," said the tale-teller. He left his satchel, still open, on the table.

The thief snatched the silver stone and slipped it into the leather bag that hung from his belt. He glanced around, grabbed a handful of other stones and slithered into the night.

The tale-teller, returning with a frosty tankard, saw him go. He stroked his beard and sighed.

Soon the thief arrived at the home of a jeweler.

"What would you give me for this?" he asked, reaching into his pouch. Feeling the largest stone, he pulled it out.

"Nothing," said the jeweler. "Common stones such as this can be found alongside any road."

"What?!" said the thief. He peered at the stone in the candlelight. He could have sworn it was silver, but now it looked like an ordinary rock.

He turned the pouch over and dumped out all the stones. Every one of them was a common pebble.

"I don't understand," said the thief, "In the tale-teller's hands, these stones were different!"

"Ah, so that's what happened," said the jeweler. "These are story stones. They can't be sold. Did you listen to the stories?"

The thief shook his head.

"Without the stories, they're completely worthless," said the jeweler. "Go on your way. I'm going to bed."

Back at the hall, the tale-teller had returned, and the listeners were again begging for a tale. What to tell? His eyes scanned the room, and met the eyes of a young maiden with an apron full of food. I know what she needs to hear, he thought. Ah, here's the perfect stone ... a heart-healing tale.

"In a certain time, in a certain place, there lived a peasant girl ..."

His eyes never left those of the maiden.

She needs this story, he realized. She needs this story even more than I do.

When the tale was done, the girl moved through the crowd until she stood before him.

"Would you come to my house and tell my sister that story?" she begged.

He looked at her a moment, then picked up the stone again and placed it in her hand.

"I think you need to be the one to tell it," he said.

The girl hurried home, with her apron full of food and the stone clutched tightly in her hand. Her sister was lying in bed, feverish and weak.

"I've brought you something wonderful," said the girl, opening her hand.

Oh no! This was a plain, ordinary rock!

Quickly she closed her hand to hide it. She would have to pretend. She placed her hand over her heart and took a deep breath.

Suddenly her mind was flooded with images, feelings ... everything that had been in the story!

"In a certain time, in a certain place, there lived a peasant girl ..."

She stumbled over some of the words, but the images remained, and she found new words. Her eyes never left her sister.

When she finished, her sister's face was radiant. "Oh, what a beautiful story. Could you tell it again?"

"Of course." The girl put the stone over her heart again, and again the images washed over her. The words came easier this time.

"This is better nourishment than food," said her sister. "Again ... please?"

Through the night, the story was told again and again, each time more smoothly. When the morning sun came through their window, it shone on two sleeping girls.

And in the hand of one of them was a stone of bright, shining gold.

The Tale – Teller, by Leslie Slape www.leslieslape.com

The Coaching Agreement

Any coaching relationship involves the Coach and the Client coming to an agreement around the nature and the details of the coaching process. Often this is a written agreement signed by both parties, a legal document developed with industry norms and standards in mind.

One of the more creative ways to reach agreement in the coaching relationship is by telling our story; we do this in our introductory conversations and in our first sessions.

In order to establish the coaching agreement we must be mindful of how our 'story' deals with the following:

- **Our education, background and experience**

I always tell people how in most countries around the world you can just read a book, put a sign up on the wall and open up your coaching practice. I'm a real stickler for education, certification and showing quality and return of investment in all that you do. So your story should truly reflect what you have acquired in education and experience that proves the quality of coaching skills that you can offer. Your story has the proof of your commitment to your profession and the value you can give your clients.

- **What we bring to the coaching process (tools, methodologies)**

There really are a million coaches out there, but your unique approach should be part of your story. It is what differentiates you. The tools and methodologies that you have chosen in your process are the essence of what you offer your clients and your story should express that.

- **Our outlook, beliefs, value system**

Your beliefs and values are always expressed in your story. If you listen carefully to the stories around you, people 'tell' in line with their values. When you become clear about your story, your values and beliefs emerge. This is part of the agreement that you create with your client.

- **Our coaching style**

Tell the story of your coaching style. It will attract those clients that you are meant to work with. It is a part of the coaching agreement.

We must also be clear and focused about:

- Managing our client's (and our own) expectations

- The roles of both coach and client

- Understanding our own limitations and boundaries in the coaching relationship (for example, availability – if we provide support outside of coaching hours)

When we meet with new or prospective clients, we tell the story that describes how we see our coaching practice. Our story presents the terms of the coaching agreement we look to achieve with our clients. It is through this 'storytelling' that we can determine if we have a suitable match between our own style and methods and the needs of our prospective client.

Together, the coach and client then create a story that describes their specific coaching agreement, terms and relationship. This is the start of the roadmap that will guide the coaching process.

TRY THIS!

(Exercise)

In your coaching practice what method do you use to come to an established agreement with your client?

What terms need to be in place for you to commit to working with a client?

What story are you telling your prospective clients? How do you tell this story?

Excerpt from a Story Coach's Journal

I had just finished my coach training and earned my qualification. I was ready to set up shop. I had even practiced my 'elevator speech' so that I could instantly explain to people what I do. And they would be mesmerized and want to come to me for coaching straight away!

I never imagined that the first time I would get to tell my elevator speech would actually be in an elevator! I never imagined that when I was asked what I do, that I would not realize that this was the opportunity to say the 4 well-practiced sentences that would guarantee me a client! I never imagined that I could just tell a story and that it might have an even better effect!

Here's what happened. I walked out of the conference during the first break and decided to step outside to get some fresh air. I walked to the elevator and the gentleman who waited beside me introduced himself and asked me where I was from. As we stepped into the elevator I replied, "Are you going to ask if I come here often too?!"

We laughed at the clichés and then I told him my story, how I was born in Ireland, and had traveled a lot, and had finally settled here.

I told him the story of how I had arrived at coaching, had worked in corporate for many years and was now going out on my own. And then he told me his story.

It was an amazing exchange of histories, education, experience and personalities...and a fascinating story.

Jim did not become my client, nor I his, but we did manage to connect quickly and deeply because we both dared to brave vulnerability and tell our stories. The more we tell our stories authentically, the more we connect with others.

We have stayed in contact throughout the years and continue to refer clients to each other.

CHAPTER 4 –

Is that Story True? Ethics and Standards in Storytelling and Coaching

* * *

"Storytelling is by far the most underrated skill in business."

— *Gary Vaynerchuck, @garyvee, Author of "Crush It!"*

The Magic Lake

Long ago, the land that today we call Ecuador was part of a rich and prosperous Inca Kingdom. But the ruling emperor was sad because his only son had fallen ill. None of the doctors could help this boy, and his father was worried that he might die. He went to the temple and prayed to the Gods.

"Oh, Great Ones, I pray to you, please make my son strong and healthy so that one day he can rule my people when I am gone."

Suddenly a voice came out of the fire burning before the altar. And it said,

The young prince must drink water from the Magic Lake, the lake at the end of the world, where the sky touches the water. The prince can be cured only with water from the Magic Lake.

The fire flamed up brightly and then it sputtered out. And there in the ashes lay a golden flask.

The old emperor was too old to journey to the end of the world. And his son was too sick. So the emperor sent forth a proclamation throughout the land, offering a rich reward to any person who could fill that golden flask with water from the Magic Lake.

It happened that in a valley, some distance from the emperor's palace, there lived a poor farmer, his wife, two sons, and a young daughter. And when they heard the emperor's announcement, the two sons said, "Father, let us go in search of the Magic Lake. We will help the prince and bring back the reward."

The father agreed to let them go, but made them promise to return before the next new moon, in time to help with the harvest.

So the two sons set off together. They journeyed from one beautiful lake to another. But nowhere could they find the Magic Lake, where the sky touches the water. And they kept watching the moon. When they saw that it was almost new again, they knew it was time to return to their father as they had promised. So they sat down and they thought what they would do.

And the younger brother said to the older, "I know what we can do. We can fill our jars with this water right here. They'll never know the difference. Surely the emperor will reward us for our trouble."

So the two boys went to the emperor, and they said they had water from the Magic Lake, even though this was a lie. When the sick prince was given a sip of it, he became no better.

Then one of the doctors said, "The water must be put into the golden flask." But when they brought the flask, a very strange thing happened. When the water was poured onto the golden flask, POUF! It vanished. The doctor said, "The flask is telling us that the brothers have lied, for it will accept only water from the Magic Lake, the lake at the end of the world, where the sky touches the water."

The emperor was so angry he ordered that the boys be thrown to into prison. Once again the message went forth through the land, calling for someone to bring the precious water.

When the father of the two boys heard what had happened to his sons, he was ashamed that his boys had lied. But then his little daughter, whose name was Sumac, stepped forward.

"Father, please let me go. I will find the Magic Lake. And perhaps I can save my brothers."

And the father said, "No, my little Sumac, you are too young." But she begged and pleaded, and finally her mother interceded on her behalf. At last the father gave his permission. "After all," he said, "we must think of our emperor and the sick prince."

Sumac was excited to be setting out on this journey. Her mother gave her a woolen bag filled with toasted kernels of corn to eat along the way. And she had for company her pet llama who also carried her provisions.

She'd gone only a little way when she saw a flock of birds pecking in a stony field. She felt sorry for them because they looked so hungry. So she threw them a handful of her corn.

That first night she curled up next to her llama under the overhang of a great rock. But all through the night she heard the hungry cry of the puma cat. She became afraid it would creep up and attack her llama. So she sent the llama home, and the next night she slept alone, hidden high up in the branches of a tree where the puma cat could not find her.

The following morning, she woke up to ...the sound of voices? When she opened her eyes, she found that she was surrounded by birds. Amazingly, she could understand all they were saying.

One bird said, "This is the same girl who gave us corn when we were so hungry."

And another said, "Poor child, she will never find the Magic Lake she is seeking."

And another said, "But of course we could help her."

Hearing this, Sumac sat up and said, "Oh, please help me! My brothers are in prison and the emperor's son is sick. Someone must go to the Magic Lake!"

The birds agreed. Each one reached under a wing and brought forth a special feather and gave it to Sumac. They told her to take the feathers and make a magic fan. They said that this would protect her in times of danger, taking her wherever she wished to go.

One bird also warned her that she would have to face many dangers at the Magic Lake. He said, "Be brave. And the fan will help you."

Sumac thanked the birds for all their help.

Then she held up the fan and said, "I wish I were at the Magic Lake!" In an instant, a soft breeze lifted her gently out of the tree, up, up into the sky, out over the mountain peaks. And it set her down on the shore of a beautiful lake.

She realized that this must be the Magic Lake because here the sky touched the water. But what could she use for a container? Then she had an idea. She held up her magic fan and said, "I wish I had a jar." Then, Ping! The golden flask itself appeared at her feet.

Sumac went to the water's edge and began filling the flask when suddenly a strange voice ordered, "Leave the water alone!" She turned, and to her horror she saw an enormous hairy-legged crab, nearly the size of a pig, coming after her. Quickly she held up her fan. And the crab fell asleep.

No sooner had she quelled one danger when another appeared, this time a huge toothy alligator that emerged from the water and was coming straight for her, warning, "Leave the water alone!" But once again, when she held up the fan, the alligator also toppled over and sank out of sight.

Then there was a shrill screech from above and Sumac looked up to see a winged serpent descending from the sky, fire spitting from its eyes, shrieking, "Sssstay away, stay away, leave the water alone!" For a third time she raised her fan and the serpent fell to the shore, stunned and powerless.

Now, finally she could fill the flask without difficulty. As soon as this was done, she held up her fan and wished herself back at the emperor's palace. In a blink, there she was, in the very room where the prince laid spread out on the bed, pale and lifeless, the doctors standing beside him.

Sumac went to his side and poured a sip of the water into his mouth. At once the prince opened his eyes, and the color came back into his cheeks. He sat up in his bed and drank some more.

The emperor was overjoyed by his son's recovery. He offered Sumac any reward she could name.

Sumac said, "I desire only three things. First, I want my brothers to be set free. When they lied about the water, it was only because they wanted so much to succeed. They meant no harm."

The emperor agreed.

"Next," said Sumac, "I want my parents to be given a farm all their own, with herds of llamas and vicunas and alpacas to graze there. That way they will never be poor again." The emperor agreed to this as well. "And what is your third wish?" he asked.

"My third wish is for the feathers of my fan to be returned to the birds who gave them to me," As soon as she said this, the feathers floated out of her hand, out the window.

"But won't you stay here and live with us at the palace?" said the emperor.

"Oh no," said Sumac. "You are very kind. But my place is with my parents and my brothers. They will be missing me."

So Sumac said good-bye to the emperor and his son. And when she reached home she found that the royal workers had already arrived and were beginning construction of a fine new house and barn. That night, she and her brothers celebrated with their parents, rejoicing that the family was together again. She was also happy to be with her llama again. They all stayed up late into the night, hearing of Sumac's journey to the Magic Lake and how she had brought back the healing waters to cure the emperor's son.

Retold by Cristy West by kind permission

Is it true?

Anyone who has read or told stories to children will be familiar with the question – is that story true? Truth in storytelling (and life!) depends on the perspective of the storyteller. In coaching, we need to understand our client's 'truth' and that forms the basis of truthful storytelling in the context of this specific coaching relationship.

As an attempt to understand truth in Story Coaching, we must examine our own honesty and authenticity making sure that we are aligned with our clients and truly invested in truth telling as part of our coaching style.

Whenever I tell stories to children, there is always one, and often several little faces that look up in wonder and ask me, "Is that true?" And when I tell stories to adults, there is usually someone who will look at me questioningly and say, "Really? Did that really happen?" No matter what I tell, I always say, "Yes, of course, it's a true story!" I say it playfully as I invite my listeners into the possibility of imagination and an abstract definition of truth! But, really, I mean it. All my stories are true. But what kind of truth is that?

Well, here's what I mean.

All stories derive from some kind of experience. They derive from an emotional response to something. They are a response to some kind of truth. Even fairytales and folklore come from a lovingly held belief, or a fear, or a special lesson that needs to be passed on to the next generation. These are all truths.

And then someone will say, but there's no such thing as a giant flying snake. And I suggest to them....maybe, one day, long, long ago there was a really big snake. It was so much bigger than any snake that anyone in the village had ever seen that they began to talk of it as a 'giant'. And maybe one day, a young man from the village saw this enormous snake in a tree. When the snake slithered to the ground, it almost seemed like it was flying. And bingo, a generation later we have a giant, flying snake!

Truth in Storytelling and Story Coaching is all about **intention and presence**.

Using stories with **intention** means –

- Honest motivation – you understand why you are telling the story and what you want to 'say' in the telling. Your motivation is clear and clean and serves the listener.

- Clear focus – you have done the work on your story, you know what the main message is that you want to deliver and it is crystal clear.

- Striving for a positive outcome (and this does not necessarily mean a happy end) – you tell a story to inspire and instill positive energy; your story may have a sad ending but is still empowering the listener.

Truthful **Presence** is about –

- Not hiding yourself within the story – you need to show up; you need to understand who you are as the teller and as the coach.

- Being your full self – not only do you not hide your talents, you show your brilliance in your stories.

- Showing up in your true authentic way – the story is not some faked up sales copy; this is the story of who you are and what you do in the world. Authenticity in your story is priceless (more on this later!).

When we can tell a story with clear intention and full presence, this is the telling of stories that are true, and it's an essential and wonderful element of Story Coaching!

Professional Standards

Our professional responsibility includes adherence to professional standards. An example of appropriate standards are defined and described in the International Coach Federation Ethical Guidelines. These can be found on the ICF charter and website, http://www.coachfederation.org

In Story Coaching however, there is another level of professional standard and it relates to the stories we can and cannot tell (or perhaps should or should not tell).

What Stories can we tell?

There are stories that can be told in every situation, stories that are entertaining, inoffensive, enjoyable, and perhaps suggest a level of understanding or wisdom. These are the kind of stories that can establish rapport, make our clients and ourselves comfortable, and set the mood for establishing safety and trust.

So, where do these stories come from? There is a reason that fairy and folk tales have lasted through generations and cultures. They contain enormous wisdom and are wonderful material for our coaching use. Also, we can find stories in urban legends and personal experience.

What characterizes their usability in every situation is that they –

- Deal with non-controversial issues.

- Use general and often stereotypical characterizations.

- Have predictable outcomes with elements of repetition in the story.

- Use personal experience with humorous but wise outcome – we learn an important lesson from these most usable stories.

What stories should we never tell?

There are stories that may never find an appropriate audience. These stories are often controversial, express personal opinions and judgment, and often have negative outcomes. To determine whether the story should or should not be told, we must be in tune with our audience/client and sensitive to issues that the client may not yet be prepared to deal with. The key is to be in touch, at all times, with our client's agenda, and where they are at every moment. The client takes the lead and deals with issues when they are ready to do so; the stories that we choose to tell must be in line with this.

As we choose to be responsible and professional in our Coaching practice, we need to adhere to Professional Standards and this includes being sensitive to finding appropriate stories to tell.

TRY THIS!

(Exercise)

Write down the standards that are the most difficult for you to implement.

Are there stories that you think you could never tell, if so, why?

Excerpt from a Story Coach's Journal

Telling the Story & Coaching the Practice of Gratitude

In the business and art of coaching, I am often amazed by the tendency that I see in people to naturally focus on what they have not yet done or finished, while completely ignoring their amazing achievements and the blessings in their lives! What delights me each time is that when these clients are listened to and their achievements are acknowledged, they just shine and gratitude comes naturally!

How often we experience negative situations, or feel overwhelmed by political or natural disasters; most of which we have no control over, yet they have such a profound negative effect on our lives. Yet the slightest shift to acknowledge our own gifts and the gifts of others, the smallest change that celebrates the presence of now, the choice to bring gratitude into our lives as a deliberate practice, can make all the difference.

A few years ago, my partner went away for the weekend on a boy's adventure. It was something like a cross between extreme camping, survivor and scout camp! He was dismayed to discover that they would not be eating very much during their 2 day mission, that it got pretty cold at night and one of the other 'boys' snored so loudly that he woke everyone up several times each night, including himself! But he came back delighted with lots of stories he could tell and quite a few that he could not!

He also brought back a wonderful practice that he promptly introduced into our household. During our evening meal, each night, we ask each person at the table "Who would like to say thank you?" Having practiced this every night since his trip, I can tell you it usually works like this... Someone always says thank you for the food on the table, and the sunshine or rain. Someone usually says thank you for our good friends and our lovely family (and what we did with them today). Someone usually says they don't have a thank you and is reminded that even in the worst of days there is always something to be thankful for. Our littlest boy usually says, "Thank you for Mummy and thank you for Daddy…" and then he gets all shy and stops talking! And sometimes, someone at the table thanks someone else at the table for an act of kindness that they did that day.

One night, my mother, brother, one of my sisters and I celebrated my Mum's birthday. Along with a few other members of our family we celebrated over a month late. It had taken that long to find the date that we could all manage. It turned out that it was on the day that my father would have celebrated his 80th birthday (13+ years after he passed away). We had a wonderful meal and a lively chat, but we forgot to say our 'thank yous.' So I thought I would say it now. Thank you for the wonderful food on the table. Thank you for the mild evening and cool breeze. Thank you for my amazing family, each one that found the time to meet together. Thank you that I have the best memories of my dad and even though we lost him too soon, I know that I am truly blessed.

In these troubled times of horrific oil spills, environmental crises, economic uncertainty and political & humanitarian disasters, it is even more important than ever to remember that we are truly blessed and there is always something to say thank you for!

CHAPTER 5 –

Once Upon a Time – Creating a Safe Space

* * *

'If you don't know the trees you may be lost in the forest, but if you don't know the stories you may be lost in life. "

— *Siberian Elder*

The Selfish Giant

Every afternoon, as they were coming from school, the children used to go and play in the Giant's garden.

It was a large lovely garden with soft green grass. Here and there over the grass stood beautiful flowers like stars, and there were twelve peach-trees that in the spring-time broke out into delicate blossoms of pink and pearl, and in the autumn bore rich fruit. The birds sat on the trees and sang so sweetly that the children used to stop their games in order to listen to them. "How happy we are here!" they cried to each other.

One day the Giant came back. He had been to visit his friend the Cornish ogre, and had stayed with him for seven years. After the seven years were over he had said all that he had to say, for his conversation was limited, and he determined to return to his own castle. When he arrived he saw the children playing in the garden.

"What are you doing here?" he cried in a very gruff voice, and the children ran away.

"My own garden is my own garden," said the Giant; "Anyone can understand that, and I will allow nobody to play in it but myself." So he built a high wall all around it, and put up a notice-board.

TRESPASSERS
WILL BE
PROSECUTED

He was a very selfish Giant.

The poor children had now nowhere to play. They tried to play on the road, but the road was very dusty and full of hard stones, and they did not like it. They used to wander round the high wall when their lessons were over, and talk about the beautiful garden inside. "How happy we were there," they said to each other.

Then the Spring came, and all over the country there were little blossoms and little birds. Only in the garden of the Selfish Giant it was still winter. The birds did not care to sing in it as there were no children, and the trees forgot to blossom. Once a beautiful flower put its head out from the grass, but when it saw the notice-board it was so sorry for the children that it slipped back into the ground again, and went off to sleep. The only people who were pleased were the Snow and the Frost. "Spring has forgotten this garden," they cried, "so we will live here all the year round." The Snow covered up the grass with her great white cloak, and the Frost painted all the trees silver. Then they invited the North Wind to stay with them, and he came. He was wrapped in furs, and he roared all day about the garden, and blew the chimney-pots down. "This is a delightful spot," he said, "We must ask the Hail on a visit." So the Hail came. Every day for three hours he rattled on the roof of the castle till he broke most of the slates, and then he ran round and round the garden as fast as he could go. He was dressed in grey, and his breath was like ice.

"I cannot understand why the Spring is so late in coming," said the Selfish Giant, as he sat at the window and looked out at his cold white garden; "I hope there will be a change in the weather."

But the Spring never came, nor the Summer. The Autumn gave golden fruit to every garden, but to the Giant's garden she gave none. "He is too selfish," she said. So it was always Winter there, and the North Wind, and the Hail, and the Frost, and the Snow danced about through the trees.

One morning the Giant was lying awake in bed when he heard some lovely music. It sounded so sweet to his ears that he thought it must be the King's musicians passing by. It was really only a little linnet singing outside his window, but it was so long since he had heard a bird sing in his garden that it seemed to him to be the most beautiful music in the world. Then the Hail stopped dancing over his head, and the North Wind ceased roaring, and a delicious perfume came to him through the open casement. "I believe the Spring has come at last," said the Giant; and he jumped out of bed and looked out.

What did he see?

He saw a most wonderful sight. Through a little hole in the wall the children had crept in, and they were sitting in the branches of the trees. In every tree that he could see there was a little child. And the trees were so glad to have the children back again that they had covered themselves with blossoms, and were waving their arms gently above the children's heads. The birds were flying about and twittering with delight, and the flowers were looking up through the green grass and laughing. It was a lovely scene, only in one corner it was still winter. It was the farthest corner of the garden, and in it was standing a little boy.

He was so small that he could not reach up to the branches of the tree, and he was wandering all round it, crying bitterly. The poor tree was still quite covered with frost and snow, and the North Wind was blowing and roaring above it. "Climb up! Little boy," said the Tree, and it bent its branches down as low as it could; but the boy was too tiny.

And the Giant's heart melted as he looked out. "How selfish I have been!" he said, "Now I know why the Spring would not come here. I will put that poor little boy on the top of the tree, and then I will knock down the wall, and my garden shall be the children's playground forever and ever." He was really very sorry for what he had done.

So he crept downstairs and opened the front door quite softly, and went out into the garden. But when the children saw him they were so frightened that they all ran away and the garden became winter again. Only the little boy did not run, for his eyes were so full of tears that he did not see the Giant coming. And the Giant stole up behind him and took him gently in his hand, and put him up into the tree. And the tree broke at once into blossom, and the birds came and sang on it, and the little boy stretched out his two arms and flung them round the Giant's neck, and kissed him. And the other children, when they saw that the Giant was not wicked any longer, came running back, and with them came the Spring. "It is your garden now, little children," said the Giant, and he took a great axe and knocked down the wall. And when the people were going to market at twelve o'clock they found the Giant playing with the children in the most beautiful garden they had ever seen.

All day long they played, and in the evening they came to the Giant to bid him good-bye.

"But where is your little companion?" he said, "The boy I put into the tree." The Giant loved him the best because he had kissed him.

"We don't know," answered the children, "He has gone away."

"You must tell him to be sure and come here to-morrow," said the Giant. But the children said that they did not know where he lived, and had never seen him before; and the Giant felt very sad.

Every afternoon, when school was over, the children came and played with the Giant. But the little boy whom the Giant loved was never seen again. The Giant was very kind to all the children, yet he longed for his first little friend, and often spoke of him. "How I would like to see him!" he used to say.

Years went over, and the Giant grew very old and feeble. He could not play about any more, so he sat in a huge armchair, and watched the children at their games, and admired his garden. "I have many beautiful flowers," he said, "But the children are the most beautiful flowers of all."

One winter morning he looked out of his window as he was dressing. He did not hate the Winter now, for he knew that it was merely the Spring asleep, and that the flowers were resting.

Suddenly he rubbed his eyes in wonder, and looked and looked. It certainly was a marvelous sight. In the farthest corner of the garden was a tree quite covered with lovely white blossoms. Its branches were all golden, and silver fruit hung down from them, and underneath it stood the little boy he had loved.

Downstairs ran the Giant in great joy, and out into the garden. He hastened across the grass, and came near to the child. And when he came quite close his face grew red with anger, and he said, "Who hath dared to wound thee?" For on the palms of the child's hands were the prints of two nails, and the prints of two nails were on the little feet.

"Who hath dared to wound thee?" cried the Giant; "tell me, that I may take my big sword and slay him."

"Nay!" answered the child; "but these are the wounds of Love."

"Who art thou?" said the Giant, and a strange awe fell on him, and he knelt before the little child.

And the child smiled on the Giant, and said to him, "You let me play once in your garden, to-day you shall come with me to my garden, which is Paradise."

And when the children ran in that afternoon, they found the Giant lying dead under the tree, all covered with white blossoms.

Oscar Wilde

The Storytelling Revival

Over the last few years, there has been a revival of Storytelling all over the world. There is recognition that storytelling has enormous application to so many fields. Universities and Colleges are teaching Storytelling and Narrative in Law Studies and Medical Schools. Medical internships and hospitals are teaching young doctors how to tell and listen to stories. Storytelling is being recognized on the corporate level not only for Marketing and Sales but as a leadership style and for employee engagement and retention. There are more storytellers now than ever and it is no longer an activity that is targeted for children alone.

In this world of ever changing technology, sophistication and choice, people are craving the simplicity of traditional storytelling; they crave the stories, the listening and the telling. There is a void that the information age and technology cannot fill. Storytelling seems to remedy the very same void that people are looking to fill when they come to coaching.

On so many levels (individual, community and society) people are looking for a connection, a truth, a sense that their life has meaning. This is clearly expressed in the popularity and development of Coaching as a profession. It is also connected to the Storytelling revival that is underway. Annette Simmons in 'The Story Factor' says "When you tell a story that touches me, you give me the gift of human attention – the kind that connects me to you, that touches my heart and makes me feel more alive…We crave something that is real or at least feels real."

The story creates a natural order of things. Why do small children want to hear the same story again and again? And they are passionate about the order and details of the story. If you make a mistake, they will be heartbroken, correct you and make you tell the story again 'properly'. This is because in telling the story, you are creating a world that has order, clear rules and limits. They know and understand what is going to happen. It is safe, defined and presents a truth that they can grasp. They have control over this truth, this world.

Adults are no different from children in that they crave the safety and predictability that is presented in the story. Nowadays the world is not safe or predictable, or even comprehensible a lot of the time. In Storytelling we can relax in the safety and clarity of the narrative; we have some control in our stories. There is a beginning, middle and end. The story creates a truth that makes sense, feels safe and ultimately, very different from reality, it allows us have some control.

> "Something is happening in the power and practice of story; in the midst of overwhelming noise and distraction, the voice of story is calling us to remember our true selves."
>
> Christina Baldwin, "The Storycatcher"

The Safe Space

Creating a safe space is an important part of creating the coaching relationship. It is important that the client feel comfortable and learn to trust the coach. In fact, the coaching relationship is dependent upon there being trust and honesty between the coach and the client. If this is to happen, the client must feel that they are in a safe space.

How do we create a safe space?

- Ensure the space itself is private and undisturbed

- Respect time limitation sessions should start and end on time

- No mobile phone or physical interruptions

- Active Listening

Another powerful way to create the 'safe space' is through the magic of the story.

Telling a Story in a Coaching Session -

Everybody loves to hear a good story. As you start to tell a story you can see the physical and emotional shift that the audience experiences. Your listener is led into a different world, the world of story and it is evocative and exciting! When you tell a story (particularly fairy and folktales), the client is gently drawn into a world that is also safe, predictable and secure.

Through storytelling the Coach acquires a powerful tool to offer, or describe, a level of understanding, or awareness, which may be inaccessible to the client. This level may be blocked for many reasons; through listening to a story, the client can hear and subsequently deal with more difficult issues.

Listening to our Client's Story in a Coaching Session -

"It is the listening for the meaning behind the story, for the underlying process, for the theme that will deepen the learning. The coach is listening for the appearance of the client's vision, values, purpose…"

- Co-Active Coaching

As we listen carefully to our client's story, the safe space is created and we allow the client to really explore their values and the issues that are blocking them in their lives.

The stories we tell our clients, and the stories we listen to them tell, articulate our respect while creating mutual trust and intimacy; this is crucial to the coaching relationship and the continuity of the coaching process.

Building the Coach – Client Relationship

Storytelling and Storylistening are integral and intuitive ways to create and build the coach – client relationship. There are several important issues to recognize as we use storytelling in this way:

Recognizing the Narrative Comfort Zone –

As we build the Coach/Client relationship we learn to recognize the narrative that is comfortable for our clients. Some clients will be more reserved and private in the stories they tell; while others will appreciate a more direct approach. As we listen attentively to our clients and the stories that they tell, they guide us to the stories that we can use that will be more useful and meaningful for our clients. We learn the stories that our clients can relate to; the stories that will really affect them.

Acknowledging and Allowing for Powerful Storytelling in Coaching –

Once our clients get used to the language of storytelling as a coaching theme or methodology, we can explore new areas and issues for our clients through story.

When we tell a fictional story, a distance exists between the listener and the story. It is not the direct experience of the listener. And though it may relate closely to the listener's experience, the distance allows a certain safety for the listener. As a result, the listener can start to consider issues, look at them more closely and more directly through the story than if you were to approach the issue in conversation. The story, once heard, does its work in time. The listener/client walks away with the story in mind, and may think about the issue in the context of the story again and again. And so the work begins. Once our clients are comfortable with thinking about the issue in the context of the story, they can then start thinking about the issue and dealing with it more directly for themselves.

The Personal Story –

In coaching, when we tell personal stories we create a wonderful opportunity to demonstrate personal integrity, honesty and sincerity. In addition, when we tell a personal story with strong client-serving intention, we connect with our clients on an emotional level. They recognize themselves in us. We connect because of the mutual story experience.

This is critical in building up the coach/client relationship and setting the ground for valuable self-discovery work.

TRY THIS!

(Exercise)

What story do you know (or have you found) that could be used to create a safe space?

What other methods do you rely on to create safety and build your relationship with your client?

Excerpt from a Story Coach's Journal

We had been walking for about an hour, the mosquitoes were biting, the sun was getting hotter, sweaters shed, and the kids were getting tired. We stopped for what I always call 'the incentivizers' – the cool water, piece of fruit, a cookie and a story! Then, re-energized, we headed up the hill at the top of which we could finally see 'the magic glen!'

"Why is it called the magic glen," my son asked. "Well, lots of reasons," I replied. "Firstly, it's an amazing place, right?" "Yes," they enthused and said, "just in this one place there are the slippery slides with the rope, the clay hill and…" I continued, "Most people don't know this valley is here, it's as if when we go away, it disappears… it's its own special magic."

As a parent, I have found that the more I tell my kids stories, the more they invite possibility, adventure, imagination and joy into their lives.

As a coach, I am completely convinced that the more I tell my clients stories, and listen to their stories, the better I coach and the more value my clients receive.

Storytelling is incredibly effective in strengthening the coaching relationships.

We left the magic glen and headed back towards where we had parked the car. There were wild flowers everywhere and I had my youngest on my shoulders feeling like a sack of potatoes, floppy from tiredness, ready for his midday sleep. The bigger boys ran on ahead, racing to get back with their seemingly endless energy and enthusiasm, especially when ice-cream might be on the cards!

As I draw this to a close, I know that you may remember that storytelling builds relationships. You probably won't remember its' advantages in parenting and coaching. But I'm sure you'll remember the Magic Glen and the boys running home with the promise of ice-cream.

We always remember the story!

CHAPTER 6 –

A long, long time ago, or maybe yesterday – Creating 'presence' in Coaching

* * *

"Your own words are the bricks and mortar of the dreams you want to realize. Your words are the greatest power you have. The words you choose and their use establish the life you experience."

~ Sonia Choquette

The Picture of Peace

There was once a king who offered a prize to the artist who could paint the best picture of peace.

Many artists tried. The king looked at all of the pictures. After much deliberation he was down to the last two. He had to choose between them.

One picture was of a calm lake. The lake was a perfect mirror for the peaceful mountains that towered around it. Overhead, fluffy white clouds floated in a blue sky. Everyone who saw this picture said that it was the perfect picture of peace.

The second picture had mountains too. These mountains were rugged and bare. Above was an angry gray sky from which rain fell. Lightning flashed.

Down the side of the mountain tumbled a foaming waterfall. This did not appear to be a peaceful place at all. But, when the king looked closely, he saw that behind the waterfall was a tiny bush growing in the rock. Inside the bush, a mother bird had built her nest. There, in the midst of the rush of angry water, sat the mother bird on her nest. She was the perfect picture of peace.

The king chose the second picture. "Because," he explained, "peace is not only in a place where there is no noise, trouble, or hard work. Peace is in the midst of things as they are, when there is calm in your heart. That is the real meaning of peace."

I heard this story from Suzi Wolf, Storyteller – Thank you!

Presence in Storytelling and Coaching

The great storytellers always say that as a storyteller, if you really see the story, your listener will see it too; if you are truly present in the telling, the audience is with you there too.

In coaching, being truly present for your client is the optimum state. You need to be with the client wherever they are; it is only then that you can accompany them on the coaching journey. By being fully present and fully conscious of this state, you can demonstrate openness, flexibility and be confident in the coaching process.

The skills required to be fully present for your client, both in storytelling and coaching are:

- <u>Active and Affective Listening</u> – listening consciously, openly and obviously to really hear your client, identify and understand his/her concerns at any given time.

- <u>Inquiry Process</u> – Encourage your client to constantly self-inquire by using tools of inquiry.

- <u>Powerful Questioning</u> - asking powerful questions that allow your client to reach a deep level of awareness and understanding.

Story Elements for Powerful Story Coaching Presence

You can help your client shift perspectives really easily when you use Storytelling in Coaching. As you tell the story, the client is drawn in to the character and his/her journey; at first it seems separate, even distant to the client's predicament. In time they can see the relationship to their own situation and this presents options that they may never have been open to consider before. By creating an alternative world or reality through our stories, we allow our clients to experiment with new possibilities for action and change.

Elements of Story

If we examine the nature of the stories we tell and those that our clients tell, we learn a huge amount about the deeper significance of the stories chosen. There is no chance involved in story choice. There is always a reason that we are drawn to a story and compelled to tell it. It is this 'reason' that is the gift of a lot of information as to the storyteller's state of mind and perception of reality. It is crucial information for the coaching process. To examine the stories we can look at all the different story elements.

Stories have very specific elements or characteristics that are the root of their power and influence. When we break down these elements and look at them closely, we learn to recognize and optimize these elements to use in coaching. This is one of the key activities of Story Coaching – to understand the elements of story that make it so powerful.

Character Creation and Development

Aside from the protagonist, there are many characters in stories that reflect the people and relationships that all listeners are familiar with. Annette Simmons in 'The Story Factor' says, *"There are a few archetypal characters that sum up many of our life stories. The hero, magician, sage, king, queen, heretic, martyr, and traveller are but a few. Although no one role can possibly explain a person's life, these stories are incredibly useful in identifying behaviour patterns."*

The characters in stories also represent social norms and behaviors in the world created by the story. Through our characters we can live an alternative life making choices that in our real lives we may have difficulty making. Our characters represent opportunities for self-realization. When we and our clients understand this, we can use our stories as a vehicle for change; our characters facilitate the change that we desire for ourselves and as we understand this, we can make it happen for real!

The Journey

When Little Red Riding Hood set out to visit her sickly grandmother, she prepared her basket of goodies and set out on the journey.

When Snow White was taken into the forest by her wicked stepmother's huntsman to be killed, she also began her great journey into the unknown.

Even Shrek (in each movie) faced a formidable journey before he could get to where he needed to be.

The truth is that every good story has a journey and it plays a very important role in the narrative structure and also in the personal development of the character.

So what is the role of the journey in our stories? Well, the journey is a metaphor for transformation. The protagonist of the story undergoes some kind of change which is enabled by the physical movement of the journey. This transformation can be physical, emotional or intellectual but it is described through the journey in the narrative form.

When I was 18, I left home and went to university overseas. It was my first time living away from home and leaving the shelter of my family and the community I grew up in. My journey had immense significance in terms of the personal process I went through. Even the journey itself can be viewed on several levels. There was the part of the journey that took place in the first 24 hours after I left home. The flights, the baggage handling, the arrival and the confusion all added to the discomfort and metaphorical severing of Lisa, the child, from home and family and being catapulted into adulthood.

I believe that the journey went way beyond the first 24 hours of physically and literally leaving home, and flying overseas. The journey continued over the next 12 months of my university program, living in dorms and meeting people from all over the world. The journey continued with the learning of how to shop, budget and cook for myself for the first time. It continued when I ran out of money, worked waitressing and cleaning houses to get by, and not have to ask my parents for support. The journey continued as I realised what I wanted to study and moved into the degree program that was offered in another town that I had to move to. In some sense, the journey continues as my life unfolds.

The coaching process is often described as a journey.

The assumption being that the client when committing to the coaching process undertakes a life-changing journey, from which she/he will emerge changed (hopefully, for the better!). Just as we are the protagonist in our life stories, the coaching journey is the vehicle of change for our protagonist, the client. As we enable our clients to take action, this movement creates a momentum which enables further action. The outcome is the coaching journey which facilitates reaching goals and creating the life that we dream of.

There is an immediate link between our stories and the coaching process. When we use story, the metaphor is clear and useful to help our clients take those first crucial steps on their journey to self-realization and fulfilment.

As we learn to examine our stories and identify our journey in them, we become better equipped to see the movement and transformation as inspiring and empowering.

TRY THIS!

(Exercises)

What do you hear when you listen actively to your client's story?

What are powerful questions? Give some examples of how you can use powerful questions.

Describe the 'characters' you have encountered in your place of work. What role do they play in your story?

Think of a journey you have taken. Write it down as a brief story.

Excerpt from a Story Coach's Journal

The Journey

I disappeared for a week.

It was intentional though I had hoped to leave some signs of life while I was gone.

But life rushed me out the door, to the airport and on a surprisingly full plane from Israel to Turkey. I travelled to join an International Women's Sailing Week. A phenomenal initiative of the Turkish conceived and run Women's Sailing School, which brings together women from all over the world to celebrate the beauty of the region and the joy of sailing – women only. Traditionally quite a macho sport, the woman owner (who's surname is the Turkish word for the 'North West Wind,' which happily we experienced quite a few times during the week as it filled our sails and kept us busy on board!) created a place where women can learn to sail and qualify as skippers, a place where we can celebrate the many faces of our strength. This week was witness to such display!

The week was simply amazing. I reconnected with sea living (memories of days and adventures gone by!), I reconnected with the simplicity of life without kids, partner and a hectic work schedule; I reconnected with wonderful friends and of course, with myself.

I was romanced by the good food, sunshine, powerful winds, beautiful sea life and the company of wonderful women. What more can a girl ask for!

Every day started with yoga and a hike, by which time it was so hot we dived into the amazingly blue and clear water to cool down and pique our appetite for breakfast. After eating fruit, yogurt and muesli, or sometimes the fresh bread baked by the local women and delivered by little boats that pulled up alongside ours, we rested, tidied up the boat and set sail. Some days the sea was quiet and we were forced to stop at the most beautiful sheltered bays for swim and snorkel. Other days the winds were so strong that we had to wear harnesses and life jackets. As we used to say in Dublin, the crack was mighty (that means we had such a great laugh!) and as only girls know how to do, discussed everything under the sun, and lots more too!

Sometimes we need to get away physically, to surround ourselves with the ideal scenario to recreate our own story of who we are in the world. To peel away all the responsibilities, those that we have chosen and those that have chosen us, so that we can reconnect to our essence and begin to see the way forward.

Sometimes it is the journey itself that delivers the learning. The hero's journey starts so simply, the willingness to set out to an adventure and be prepared for all that you will face.

Without a doubt, you will become changed; perhaps enriched and fulfilled, perhaps with a new awareness and understanding. You will be changed though, possibly forever!

CHAPTER 7 –

... in a country far, far away – just around the corner – Elements of Story Enhancing the Coaching Process

* * *

"Sometime reality is too complex. Stories give it form. "

— *Jean Luc Godard -French Filmmaker*

The Sesame Seed

There was once a king who often sailed up and down the Nile. One day while returning to port, he saw a fisherwoman knee deep in the water, casting out her nets. She was not the most beautiful woman he had ever seen, but something about her struck him. Later the king could not get the woman out of his mind. He sent his advisor to find out whether she was single, married, or widowed.

The advisor returned saying, "The woman is married to a fisherman, and though he is poor, he is thought well of by his neighbors."

"What a shame," said the king.

The advisor said, "Don't be discouraged. You are the king, and can have whatever, or whomever you want. If your conscience allows, there are ways to get rid of the husband." The two put their heads together and devised a plan.

The next day the king sent for the husband. "Fisherman," he said, "I shall ask something of you, and if you don't succeed, I'll have your head chopped off. You must come before me tomorrow riding and walking."

"At the same time?" asked the fisherman.

"Yes, at the same time!" snapped the king.

The fisherman went home and told his wife the whole puzzling story. "It's truly a paradox," said the husband. "How can I ride and walk at the same time?"

"Don't worry," said the wife. She went off to take counsel with her sister.

"Borrow my she-goat," said the sister. "Tell your husband to go to the palace with his back-side planted on the she-goat's back, and his feet dragging on the ground."

When the king saw the man coming to court both walking and riding he knew he'd been outsmarted. "Well, fisherman," he said, "I'm going to require another task. Tomorrow you must appear before me dressed naked."

The distraught fisherman went home and told his wife that being dressed naked was a great paradox, truly impossible. "Don't worry," said the wife, and she went to take counsel from her sister.

The sister said, "Tell your husband in the morning instead of putting on clothes, he must drape a fishing net over his shoulders." This is exactly what the fisherman did.

When the king saw the fisherman dressed naked, he realized the fisherman understood paradox, and that the third and final task must be truly impossible. "Fisherman," he said, I want you to bring to the court, an infant who tells riddles and tall tales. If you fail, I'll have your head."

The fisherman went home and in great distress said to his wife, "Now I'm done for. Where on earth is there an infant who can tell riddles and tall tales?"

"I don't know," said the wife, "but I shall ask my sister."

After hearing the third task, the sister said, "There is but one class of infant who can tell tall tales and riddles, and that in one who is half jinn and half human. There just happens to be such an infant in a nearby town."

So the next morning the fisherman went before the king holding the seven-day-old infant in his arms. "You expect this one to tell riddles and tall tales?" bellowed the king.

The fisherman said nothing, but the infant called out, "Peace be on you, Oh Great King." The king was taken aback, and the infant began his tall tale. "I'm a well-to-do fellow and there's how I got my wealth. Fifty years ago I was poor and hungry. I stood beneath a date palm heavily laden with fruit. I tossed clods of dried earth trying to knock the dates down. But the dates held fast. Those dates were sticky as dates will be, and the dirt held fast to the dates, until there was nearly an acre of land up there in the tree."

There was nothing the king loved more than a tall tale, "That's very reasonable," he said. "Go on with the tale, little teller."

"So," said the infant, "I got a plow and an ox and a handful of sesame seeds. I climbed the tree, and plowed, and planted, and the rains came, and the crops grew, and made me a wealthy man. I bought lands and have prospered ever since. Only there is one thing bothering me."

"What's that?" asked the king.

"Since that first harvest there's been one sesame seed stuck in the bark of that date palm tree. I've been obsessed with it for fifty years. No matter how hard I poke and prod I can't get hold of it. So, Great King, here's the riddle: Should I forget about it and move on?"

The king was so delighted by the infant teller of riddles and tall tales that he cried, "Of course, clever one! You're a rich man. You'll never want for sesame seed. Forget about it!"

The infant replied, "You seem to be a wise king, so why not follow your own advice?"

"My own advice?" puzzled the king.

"Yes," cried the infant. "Your life is full of ease and pleasure. You have dozens of women showering you with affection. So forget about the one you cannot have. Let it go."

This was a king who had planned that morning to behead someone. But the infant's words went into his ears, down through his heart, and into his belly. All the way through him these words rang true. A smile came to his lips, and he said, "So be it. Go forth good fisherman and may God bless you and your wife."

And that is the tale of the king and the fisher woman, and the husband, and the sister, and the goat, and the net, and the half-jinn infant, and the sesame seed. So let us remember, my friends, when we think we cannot contend with paradox, perhaps we can. And before we go lusting after things beyond our reach, we must first take stock of the good things we already have.

From "The Moon and the Well," by kind permission of Erica Helm Meade

*A*s a Story Coach you can deepen and enhance the coaching process with the rich world of Storytelling. Each story becomes a gift, an opening into a world of creative imagination where great wonders and magic are the reality. As we look at more story elements, we learn how to create this magic and weave it into the coaching process.

Imagery

Storytelling relies on all kinds of imagery to enliven the senses and create a sense of 'reality' in the story. This includes the use of nature, cultural references, religion, magic and lots more! Using imagery during the coaching process is not only helpful, but can also be incredibly powerful when working on examining perspectives, challenging the way we look at situations and thinking about how we can reframe them.

Annette Simmons in "The Story Factor" relates to this when she says, *"A good story delivers context... People already have many stories they tell themselves to interpret their experiences."*

When the client hears a story that uses strong imagery (of any kind) it creates a context that can often access memory and individual experience. This broadens the picture for the client and creatively enriches the experience. In addition, when we look at the imagery that the client uses for describing their own stories, we can learn a lot about their perspective. Using imagery to broaden the client's view enables them to reframe their problematic issues. It is a stepping stone in the path to clarity and focus, a crucial part of the coaching process.

Secrets, Discovery

The use of secrets and discovery in storytelling deepens the plot and adds intrigue, excitement and tension to our story. The secret often has a pivotal role in a story; to understand the true motivations of characters, to uncover a previously hidden history, or to realise the true depth of certain relationships. In life, secrets usually have a similar role and they can be hugely important in the coaching process.

Both part of the storytelling world and the nature of humankind, secrets weave in and out of our lives and our stories. Secrets can be an aid to survival and they can be the root of the greatest anxiety and stress. Through the coaching process we need to help the client uncover their own secrets, and in doing so they can discover their own truth in relation to the secret. This discovery is crucial in the process of resolving issues that have been creating all kinds of blocks in their lives. And in resolving these issues, the result is enormous empowerment for the client (and often the coach too!).

Here are two examples:

1. *The Client revealed the secret that her husband was having an affair. This was only the first of her 'secrets' - she had known of the situation, but was in denial. She secretly felt that somehow it was her fault; that she had encouraged him to stray and almost believed he was justified because she had lost interest in him when their babies were born (they had had 3 in quick succession). Another secret was that her father had also had an affair. These 'secrets' had allowed her to survive because her biggest fear was that if she revealed all, she would fall apart and lose everything.*

2. *Secrets in Organizations – The Client asks himself, "How can I be a manager when there are so many secrets? When I may have to fire 30% of my team, when I don't know all the answers, when I feel like I might want to leave the organization? What kind of stories do I tell when I have a lot of secrets and I want and need to keep them?"*

It is important to note that acknowledging and working through secrets does not mean that the secret no longer exists, or that the client has to tell the world everything. It means that we acknowledge the role that secrets play in our story and become purposeful about their role in our life and work.

Conflict & Resolution

The role of conflict in stories is to provide the catalyst through which our protagonists learn the required lesson and prove themselves by finding the creative and often unexpected resolution. The conflict itself is a source of dramatic tension and seems, to the listener, impossible to resolve. The listener wonders what the characters in the story will do in relation to this conflict. This is the big mystery of the story and, in fact, of human nature. What do we choose to do in the face of conflict? How will we behave? Will we be honourable? What will motivate us and how will we find resolution?

The conflict is the meat of the story, the main reason that the narrative works. What kind of story would Romeo and Juliet have been if the families were the best of friends? What would we tell about Sleeping Beauty if her godmother had loved and cherished her, and not been wicked at all? Would we be interested in Little Red Riding Hood at all if there was no wolf in the story? Once the conflict has been established then the full potential of the story and the characters exist.

In coaching, the client identifies the conflict in their lives. By examining this conflict, the client can examine more closely the elements in life that are creating a block, or stopping them from reaching their full potential.

The story resolution usually shows the protagonist triumphing against all odds. The conflict resolution delights the listener in its exquisite fairness, a just ending to the trials and tribulations of our hero! Love wins out; the poor hardworking soul inherits or earns a fortune; the king learns his lesson and becomes good.

In coaching, we can use storytelling as a wonderful metaphor for our clients. They can face their own conflicts and find creative and just resolutions. They deserve the very same opportunities for a just and promised future; they can also create their dreams and realise their potential. And using story allows them to dare to do so!

Lessons Learnt

Many traditional stories, folklore and folktales, were told for the purpose of the moral. The moral of the story taught the important lesson that needed to be passed on through the generations. Similarly, we can use storytelling in coaching to help pass on those important lessons. What better way to share wisdom than to do so through the most powerful of mediums, the story.

Often the lesson of the story is the very lesson that the coaching client has difficulty hearing or understanding. By using the story, we can give our clients exposure to the lessons that they may need to hear, but are unable to do so. As they hear the story, the lesson sinks in and slowly the client begins to relate it to their own personal situation. The wisdom of the story can teach in a subtle and powerful way, and penetrate deeply but gently. So in using storytelling, the coach can suggest solutions and options that may otherwise be inaccessible to the client.

Stephen Denning in 'Storytelling in Organizations-Why Storytelling is Transforming 21st Century Organizations and Management' (2005) says,

> "Storytelling is like a dance, in which I invite the listeners to come with me, arm-in-arm, and together we explore a story... together and co-creating the setting and the trajectory of the story. Whether anything comes of it will depend, not on the story that I tell, but rather on the story that the listeners tell themselves. It is their own story that will be liberating, energizing, and exciting."

TRY THIS!

(Exercise)

What is the main conflict in your story right now? Are there any secrets hidden within this conflict? Create a story rich with imagery to imagine a resolution. It does not have to be realistic, play with it and you might be surprised what you come up with!

Excerpt from a Story Coach's Journal

I keep seeing hitch-hikers. It's like when you buy a red umbrella, the first you've ever seen in your life, and then every day for the next week you see them everywhere. Or when you think you might be pregnant and then everywhere you look you see women waddling by with a huge tummy and that excited expectant look!

So, everywhere I look I keep seeing hitch-hikers. I know it's the height of summer and everyone is travelling, but it has stirred in me something quite unexpected!

I look at the young, handsome, excited travelers and I can't help but feel a warm, mushy, longing feeling, actually this is the mild description. This evening as I drove to a meeting in the dusk, I felt an intense longing to be that young and handsome again; to be care-free with a backpack on my back and my thumb out waiting for the ride that will take me wherever I decide to go at that very moment!

Lucy and I arrived at the station in Sienna just in time to catch the train to Venice. We were very excited. Even though we had been travelling for several weeks, Venice was the place that we had been aiming for, for quite some time. And the film festival was just about to start. The train ran through the night and we arrived in Venice station at some ungodly hour. It was too late to find a hostel and too early to start touring, so we looked around the station until we found a waiting room where we might be lucky enough to catch a few undisturbed hours of sleep. There was one such room that was strangely empty; we walked in, grabbed a row of chairs each and both of us curled over our backpacks and fell fast asleep.

Several hours later I awoke to the sound of a man clearing his throat. I opened my eyes and did a double-take. The man sitting across from me (the throat clearer) winked at me. He was tall and blonde, probably in his seventies and wearing a huge cowboy hat; his suit was bright purple with a pink, striped shirt and I noticed his hands were perfectly manicured. The woman sitting next to him wore a mink coat from head to foot and I suspected that she wore not much underneath it. She was in her thirties I reckoned and her hand that draped over the gentleman's purple sleeve was dripping in diamonds and shocking red nails. She looked bored and stifled a yawn. I looked around the waiting room to see others in similar garb.

"Luce, Luce, wake-up!" I shook her a bit more violently than I had intended; she nearly fell of the chair.

"What is it? Where are we?" she asked.

"I dunno," I whispered, "just check out these people."

We smiled and quietly grabbed our things and walked towards the exit. There we found the red carpet and realized that we had stumbled into the waiting room of the Orient Express. It was about to leave on its latest adventure.

We were not invited to join them. However, we did manage to get a few hours of much needed sleep!

For me, travelling with a backpack, an eye for adventure and an ear for a story is what life is all about. You get to meet unexpected people, hear amazing tales and experience things you never dreamed of. Every sandwich becomes a feast; every friendly gesture fills you with gratitude, a sense of safety and well-being. The beauty of what awaits you stuns you into silence, joy and appreciation. It's always better than you imagined!

But it doesn't just have to be when you're young and travelling the world with a backpack. These sights and sounds, people and stories, gestures of good will and friendship are all around us. Usually we're too busy to notice; our schedule doesn't allow us the time to sit in a town square and watch the people. Our kids are too demanding to let us just drink another cup of coffee and chat with a stranger. But who's to say we can't just stop and do it anyway.

So, this week, I have decided to do just that. Imagine that I'm on the road again, that I don't have to drive someone somewhere, pick up this and that and make the deadline. This week I will have my virtual backpack there and ready so that I can notice the beauty all around me and take that extra moment to be thankful for my blessings. Why don't you try it too?!

CHAPTER 8 –

Break your heart laughing! – Using humour in your Stories for Coaching

* * *

"I wrote the story myself. It's about a girl who lost her reputation and never missed it. "

— *Mae West*

Three Men in a Boat

Excerpt from Chapter 1

THERE were four of us – George, and William Samuel Harris, and myself, and Montmorency. We were sitting in my room, smoking, and talking about how bad we were – bad from a medical point of view I mean, of course.

We were all feeling seedy, and we were getting quite nervous about it. Harris said he felt such extraordinary fits of giddiness come over him at times, that he hardly knew what he was doing; and then George said that HE had fits of giddiness too, and hardly knew what HE was doing. With me, it was my liver that was out of order. I knew it was my liver that was out of order, because I had just been reading a patent liver-pill circular, in which were detailed the various symptoms by which a man could tell when his liver was out of order. I had them all.

It is a most extraordinary thing, but I never read a patent medicine advertisement without being impelled to the conclusion that I am suffering from the particular disease therein dealt with in its most virulent form. The diagnosis seems in every case to correspond exactly with all the sensations that I have ever felt.

I remember going to the British Museum one day to read up the treatment for some slight ailment of which I had a touch – hay fever, I fancy it was. I got down the book, and read all I came to read; and then, in an unthinking moment, I idly turned the leaves, and began to indolently study diseases, generally. I forget which was the first distemper I plunged into – some fearful, devastating scourge, I know – and, before I had glanced half down the list of "premonitory symptoms," it was borne in upon me that I had fairly got it.

I sat for a while, frozen with horror; and then, in the listlessness of despair, I again turned over the pages. I came to typhoid fever – read the symptoms – discovered that I had typhoid fever, must have had it for months without knowing it – wondered what else I had got; turned up St. Vitus's Dance – found, as I expected, that I had that too, – began to get interested in my case, and determined to sift it to the bottom, and so started alphabetically – read up ague, and learnt that I was sickening for it, and that the acute stage would commence in about another fortnight. Bright's disease, I was relieved to find, I had only in a modified form, and, so far as that was concerned, I might live for years. Cholera I had, with severe complications; and diphtheria I seemed to have been born with. I plodded conscientiously through the twenty-six letters, and the only malady I could conclude I had not got was housemaid's knee.

I felt rather hurt about this at first; it seemed somehow to be a sort of slight. Why hadn't I got housemaid's knee? Why this invidious reservation? After a while, however, less grasping feelings prevailed. I reflected that I had every other known malady in the pharmacology, and I grew less selfish, and determined to do without housemaid's knee. Gout, in its most malignant stage, it would appear, had seized me without my being aware of it; and zymosis I had evidently been suffering with from boyhood. There were no more diseases after zymosis, so I concluded there was nothing else the matter with me.

I sat and pondered. I thought what an interesting case I must be from a medical point of view, what an acquisition I should be to a class! Students would have no need to "walk the hospitals," if they had me. I was a hospital in myself. All they need do would be to walk round me, and, after that, take their diploma.

Then I wondered how long I had to live. I tried to examine myself. I felt my pulse. I could not at first feel any pulse at all. Then, all of a sudden, it seemed to start off. I pulled out my watch and timed it. I made it a hundred and forty-seven to the minute. I tried to feel my heart. I could not feel my heart. It had stopped beating. I have since been induced to come to the opinion that it must have been there all the time, and must have been beating, but I cannot account for it. I patted myself all over my front, from what I call my waist up to my head, and I went a bit round each side, and a little way up the back. But I could not feel or hear anything. I tried to look at my tongue. I stuck it out as far as ever it would go, and I shut one eye, and tried to examine it with the other. I could only see the tip, and the only thing that I could gain from that was to feel more certain than before that I had scarlet fever.

I had walked into that reading-room a happy, healthy man. I crawled out a decrepit wreck.

I went to my medical man. He is an old chum of mine, and feels my pulse, and looks at my tongue, and talks about the weather, all for nothing, when I fancy I'm ill; so I thought I would do him a good turn by going to him now. "What a doctor wants," I said, "is practice. He shall have me. He will get more practice out of me than out of seventeen hundred of your ordinary, commonplace patients, with only one or two diseases each." So I went straight up and saw him, and he said:

"Well, what's the matter with you?"

I said:

"I will not take up your time, dear boy, with telling you what is the matter with me. Life is brief, and you might pass away before I had finished. But I will tell you what is NOT the matter with me. I have not got housemaid's knee. Why I have not got housemaid's knee, I cannot tell you; but the fact remains that I have not got it. Everything else, however, I HAVE got."

And I told him how I came to discover it all.

Then he opened me and looked down me, and clutched hold of my wrist, and then he hit me over the chest when I wasn't expecting it – a cowardly thing to do, I call it – and immediately afterwards butted me with the side of his head. After that, he sat down and wrote out a prescription, and folded it up and gave it me, and I put it in my pocket and went out.

I did not open it. I took it to the nearest chemist's, and handed it in. The man read it, and then handed it back.

He said he didn't keep it.

I said:

"You are a chemist?"

He said:

"I am a chemist. If I was a co-operative stores and family hotel combined, I might be able to oblige you. Being only a chemist hampers me."

I read the prescription. It ran:

"1 lb. beefsteak, with

 1 pt. bitter beer

every 6 hours.

1 ten-mile walk every morning.

1 bed at 11 sharp every night.

And don't stuff up your head with things you don't understand."

I followed the directions, with the happy result – speaking for myself – that my life was preserved, and is still going on.

Jerome K. Jerome

Humor is often a forgotten resource in the coaching process and can be a powerful Story Coaching approach.

The Funny Story

What is it that makes a story funny? Why do we laugh?

What is the purpose of comedy in storytelling? How can it help us in our coaching practice?

Everyone loves a good laugh and most people like to hear a funny story. It can be a wonderful tension reducer, a great way to relieve stress. When we tell a funny story, it creates a momentary break in the tension that has preceded. In addition, it can add a brand new perspective to an issue that seems rife with stress and has a negative outlook. When we hear a funny story we are reminded that there are more ways to interpret a given situation and it may not be so bad after all!

Hearing a funny story, we are endeared to the storyteller; they seem more human, likeable and interesting than previously; this makes it easier to find common ground with the person. So, humor can be an integral part of the communication process and the building of a relationship. These are all critical elements of the coaching process.

When we tell an amusing anecdote or a funny story, it reminds us to stop taking life so seriously and to see the lighter side of things. If we can see the humor in a situation, we may be able to find a previously un-thought-of solution.

There does need to be some caution taken in using humor. Not everyone finds the same things funny, but if we are sensitive to our clients' needs and responsible in terms of the issues we bring up, we can use humor in a successful and powerful way.

Humorous Approaches

There are a variety of formal ways of approaching humor. There are many humorous performances (stand-up comedians, recordings and live sessions), books, articles, etc.

Generally the benefits of laughter are widely known and written about; this is an important resource for anyone in the Coaching profession. For example –

- Laughter Therapy

- Yoga Laughter

- Improvisation and Playback Theatre

In our coaching practice it is important to treat humor as an additional resource, another item in our toolbox. Here is a simple process to introduce a lighter approach within any given coaching scenario.

4 Step Approach to Adding Play to our 'Story' –
1. **Step 1 - Breathe**
   When tension is high and a situation seems insurmountable, take a step away and breathe deeply, and then again. If we are stressed, we tend to breath in a more shallow manner and that reduces our oxygen intake. Once we breathe in a deliberate and deep way, we start to de-stress and are able to find a different approach to the issue.

2. **Step 2 - Analyze**
   Understand the root of the stress or tension; the feelings of frustration come from something specific. Understand what that is, suspend your self-judgment and begin to accept that it is okay to feel what you are feeling right now, simply because you are feeling it.

3. **Step 3 - Reframe and Play the Game!**
   Look at this situation from someone else's perspective; your partner, your colleague, your child, your parent or even your pet! When you see it from their eyes, turn it into a role-play game and start playing. Role-play out the situation; give it a couple of different solutions or endings. Then do it again.

4. **Step 4 - Retell Your Story**
   Introducing game and fun to the story makes it a whole different experience. Now tell your new story, it should be fun and light!

There are many ways to add energy, lightness and humor into your coaching and into your life – how do you do it? Here are 10 Powerful questions that you can use to do just that!

<u>10 Powerful Questions to Help Introduce Energy, Lightness and Humor into your Coaching and your Life!</u>
1. *What makes you laugh?*

2. *When was the last time you really laughed? What was the situation and who made it happen?*

3. *What are the ways that you can 'play out' your tension and stress?*

4. *Who can you emulate or learn humor from?*

5. *Who are the people in your life that make you laugh most?*

6. *Think of a funny story you heard recently; did you laugh out loud? How can you incorporate this humor into your own stories?*

7. *Do you look for ways to laugh on a regular basis?*

8. *How do you feel when you laugh out loud? How does it affect your day? How does it affect the people around you?*

9. *Is there someone in your life who always makes you laugh? Do they know it? Do you make an effort to be with them on a regular basis?*

10. *Who do you make laugh? Why do they find you funny? How do you feel when you make someone else laugh?*

Lightness and Energy

When we 'lighten' up, we see an issue as less insurmountable. We can release the tension that we have built up around the problem. This release of tension can be described as positive energy which can then be channeled into productive and positive action.

Creating lightness through storytelling is all about the type of stories we tell, and the time that we choose to tell the story. Using humor in storytelling is a wonderful way to create this lightness. In addition, many stories that have a positive and simple outcome create the 'lightening up' affect.

The story we tell ourselves can determine how light or heavy we feel about any given situation. We can change the story and the effect makes the situation much more manageable.

For example –

Suzy was terrified that her baby would get sick. He had begun to cough and sneeze and she started to imagine that the cold turned into the flu, and the flu into pneumonia. She started to worry about who would look after her other two kids while she took the baby to hospital. She was getting into a state. And then the baby sneezed again. Her 5 year old started laughing and said that the baby looks just like a frog! "A frog?" Suzy asked, "Why a frog?" Her 5 year old daughter started singing a song she had learnt about the frog that caught a cold but no one knew he was sick because he was already green! Suzy started laughing...she really was worrying for no reason. She suddenly felt so much lighter!

When we become lighter, we have more energy and that energy is a positive force. When we become lighter, we are living in the present, the here and now, and that reality is a kind of truth. When we allow laughter, energy and light into our lives we can make positive and long lasting change.

TRY THIS!

(Exercise)

Learning to laugh at ourselves is the hardest but most worthwhile lesson! Choose a personal experience from your own life and write it down. Then examine what you have written and see where you can change your perspective and make it lighter. Keep working on this story until it makes you laugh. Then tell it to someone.

Excerpt from a Story Coach's Journal

When I was young, yes I know I'm still young, but I'm talking about REALLY young, I worked on cruise ships. I spent almost a year cruising the Caribbean as a photographer; shooting, printing (in the days before digital) and selling photographs of families, couples, and fine young things out for a good time and the four "S" words- sun, sea, shopping and s... let's just say love!

The sun shines most days round the islands; they donned the latest beach fashion and strutted their stuff on the ship's promenades, the pool, casino and restaurants. They were beautiful, young men and women with sun-cream oiled skin basking in the glorious sunshine.

The sea is bluer than you can imagine, rich, deep and inviting, with the occasional appearance of smiling dolphins riding the waves of the ship passing and flying fish soaring by as we moved between the islands.

Each island greeted the ships with offers of shopping excursions, somewhat reluctant and grim-faced locals selling their wares to the holiday stricken passengers out for the best deal, something different that proved they were really there!

And the final "S" – let me tell you a story.

One evening I was invited to the ship's library to take a photograph of a group of people who wanted a special token to remember their cruise. They were a group of young couples who were celebrating theirs friend's upcoming wedding. A kind of joint bachelor and hen party over the three days of the cruise; they wanted a group shot that they could all take home from the trip. I entered the library and saw that they were in the middle of an intense conversation. I cleared my throat to draw their attention and introduced myself.

"Are you ready to take the shot?" I asked.

"Sure, yeah, let's do it," they replied.

Then one of the guys nudged the other and said "I bet she has the best answer. Let's ask her."

Then a third piped up, "We're wondering what's the wildest place that anyone has done it… you know, Dave here reckons that maybe you would have a good story to tell, I mean you have that cute Irish accent."

As I set up the group photograph, I joked with them about how much fun it was to think about the answer to their question. They were a handsome group and it was easy to take a good shot. Once I had finished they reminded me that I owed them an answer.

So I described a beautiful castle in the west of Ireland, a hike up a windswept hill, the mist lifting to reveal the breathtaking view of wild cliffs and the fierce drop to the pounding waves of the ocean below. I described how we had walked up the hill with the soft rain (a truly Irish phenomena) caressing our faces and how at the very top of the hill, we had entered the ruins of the castle. He had taken my hand and led me up to the second floor of the broken down, burnt out building…

Each person in the group, probably like you, was leaning forward in anticipation of the next words that I would say.

I smiled.

I sighed.

And I said, "There is nothing in the world more powerful than love, except perhaps, a really great story!"

I have yet to meet someone who does not like to hear a good story. Stories Empower. Stories Sell. Stories are the way we live and breathe in the world!

Next time, you need to deliver a message in a powerful way, simply tell a good story!

CHAPTER 9 –

Storytelling for developing Effective Communication Practices

* * *

"Story gives people enough space to think for themselves. A story develops and grows in the mind of your listener. If it is a good story, you don't have to keep it alive by yourself. It is automatically retold or replayed in the minds of your listeners. "

— Annette Simmons, Author of "The Story Factor"

The Cracked Pot

A water bearer in India had two large pots, each hung on each end of a pole which he carried across his neck. One of the pots had a crack in it, and while the other pot was perfect and always delivered a full portion of water at the end of the long walk from the stream to the master's house, the cracked pot arrived only half full.

For a full two years this went on daily, with the bearer delivering only one and a half pots full of water to his master's house. Of course, the perfect pot was proud of its accomplishments, perfect to the end for which it was made. But the poor cracked pot was ashamed of its own imperfection, and miserable that it was able to accomplish only half of what it had been made to do.

After two years of what it perceived to be a bitter failure, it spoke to the water bearer one day by the stream. "I am ashamed of myself, and I want to apologize to you." "Why?" asked the bearer. "What are you ashamed of?" "I have been able, for these past two years, to deliver only half my load because this crack in my side causes water to leak out all the way back to your master's house. Because of my flaws, you have to do all of this work, and you don't get full value from your efforts," the pot said. The water bearer felt sorry for the old cracked pot, and in his compassion he said, "As we return to the master's house, I want you to notice the beautiful flowers along the path." Indeed, as they went up the hill, the old cracked pot took notice of the sun warming the beautiful wild flowers on the side of the path, and this cheered it some. But at the end of the trail, it still felt bad because it had leaked out half its load, and so again it apologized to the bearer for its failure. The bearer said to the pot, "Did you notice that there were flowers only on your side of your path, but not on the other pot's side? That's because I have always known about your flaw, and I took advantage of it. I planted flower seeds on your side of the path, and every day while we walk back from the stream, you've watered them. For two years I have been able to pick these beautiful flowers to decorate my master's table. Without you being just the way you are, he would not have this beauty to grace his house."

Each of us has our own unique flaws. We're all cracked pots. But if we will allow it, the Lord will use our flaws to grace His Father's table. So, as we seek ways to minister together, and as God calls you to the tasks He has appointed for you, don't be afraid of your flaws.

Source unknown

W_{hen} you tell a story, it becomes easy to communicate a message of acceptance, positivity, and empowerment. Storytelling becomes the means for powerful communication in the Coaching process.

The Power of Storytelling

"A good story induces a form of trance. The next time you say "I want to tell you a little story..." watch what happens. People will shift around to get comfortable, lean back, open their eyes, and some will even slack their jaws. Story induces an altered state of awareness..." according to Annette Simmons in "The Story Factor".

This 'altered state of awareness' that Annette Simmons discusses, creates a phenomenal opportunity for coaching work to happen. As we tell the story, the listener opens up to the experience of the story. This, in turn, opens them up to their own stories and the possibilities that present themselves in the story space.

We have established that everyone likes to hear a good story. It is an instinctive statement similar to the belief that everyone tells stories. Life is all about our experiences and how we choose to tell them. We tell our stories during meals, at bus stops, on trains and planes, during chance meetings and in phone conversations to our best friends and partners. We tell our stories to our parents and our children, to our communities and our congregations. We tell our stories to ourselves.

What we choose to tell is entirely subjective. What we choose to tell defines the very experience that we are telling. As soon as we examine the narrative that we use, when we use inquiry to look at our narrative choices, we can begin to understand why our stories are the way they are.

You know how there is someone in each one of our lives that always tells the same old stories? You invite them for dinner and between the main course and dessert, the same conversation shows up where this friend or relative will tell that story that he always tells (often word for word!). Well, I started wondering, why is he stuck in this old story? What purpose is it serving? How could he tell the story differently?

When we inquire into our stories, we learn to retell them. This does not mean rewriting history or changing the past in any way. It's about learning to tell stores from a different perspective so that they serve and empower us.

We can choose to tell better stories!

Story Listening

In Co-Active Coaching there is an interesting reference to story:

> "It is the listening for the meaning behind the story, for
> the underlying process, for the theme that will deepen
> the learning. The coach is listening for the appearance
> of the client's vision, values, purpose'"
>
> 'Co-Active Coaching' - Whitworth, Kimsey-House,
> Kimsey-House, Sandahl

Storytelling gives the client access to a new level of understanding or awareness. Typically, a client may be experiencing being stuck or blocked in some way, the coach's role is to help them shift their perspective or reframe their reality in order to become 'unblocked.' Through storytelling, the client gets access to this shift or reframe in a gentle and subtle way. By listening to a story, the client can learn about and subsequently deal with the more difficult and deeper issues.

When we learn to listen to our client's story with attention and sensitivity, and to the minute details of their narrative, we are learning the skills of 'Active Listening' in coaching. When we listen well, we learn the narrative choices that our clients make and this tells us an enormous amount about their state of mind, life perspective and desire for and ability to change.

When we listen to our own stories, we begin to understand our own interpretation of our lives through the choice of narrative we use. This process of active listening and inquiry results in a truth and empowerment that is incredibly valuable to coaching.

Story Communication Process

Using Storytelling in coaching, we are forced to deliberately examine the language we use. When we choose to tell a story, we need to be mindful of the type of language that is in the story. This gives a wonderful opportunity to make sure that the words we use are consistent with our client's profile and state of mind. It is as if we are 'forced' to be respectful and appropriate in the language we use with our clients by the very process involved in Storytelling. We have to become truly present for our client by examining the very words we use when we choose a story to tell.

As we listen to our clients' stories, we can access their innermost state simply by examining the words they chose. As we listen closely to this narrative choice, we can hear their concerns, fears, values and beliefs.

In NLP (Neuro-Linguistic Programming), there is the concept of 'filters' which are used by people to translate their experience into perception. Sue Knight in 'NLP At Work' says, "*The filters on your experience determine how you make sense of reality... by learning to recognize these filters in yourself and others, you begin to build bridges of communication. There are no rights and wrongs about the filters... they are a part of what makes you unique.*"

The stories we tell are the perfect way of expressing our filters. Someone who tells the story of a trip through his interaction with people as opposed to someone who tells a similar story describing the places he visited – these show very apparent filters. When we understand the filters that people choose, then we can understand their perspective and tell stories that they can better relate to.

Similarly, if we are coaching face-to-face, we can read what their body language is telling us as they tell us their story. Again, the narrative choice that our client makes communicates a huge amount about them.

When we allow our clients to tell their story, and we listen to them intently and actively, we are providing the communication tool for our practice.

It is this space that allows the coach to:

- Encourage our client in their doubts, new experiences and attempts to change

- Accept them unconditionally

- Provide the emotional and physical opportunity for the client to explore their options and discovery new truths

- Reinforce them in their new experiences and thoughts

- Develop Powerful Questions

The many uses of Storytelling in Coaching create this powerful communication process and allow the coach to:

- Use respectful and appropriate language

- Summarize, paraphrase, reiterate, and mirror back to ensure clarity and understanding

- Provide clear and direct feedback to the client

- Examine and articulate new perspectives, and reframe present assumptions

- Be clear and upfront about coaching objectives

TRY THIS!

(Exercise)

Next time you are in a coaching conversation (or even with a friend) jot down some notes about their story. What additional information can you know about the other person (state of mind, perspective, and specific opinion) by listening actively to their story?

Excerpt from a Story Coach's Journal

It was incredibly hot, sauna hot; they said more than 40 degrees in the shade and the desert wind was blowing dry and sandy around me. I had packed light, but in this heat and after walking awhile, I could feel the weight on my back. I walked the way we had come, but the uniformed official told me to go back; departures were on the other side. It was sleepy in the heat and everyone seemed very relaxed, or perhaps just numbed by the hot wind. The border police checked my passport, and asked why I wasn't smiling. I said with a big smile on my face, "I'm sad to leave!" Then a young man approached me and said he was doing a survey from the tourist ministry, could he ask me a few questions.

"How long had I spent in Jordan?" "Just 24 hours," I replied. "Where did I visit?" "Aqaba," I said. "Was it business or pleasure?" "Business," I said, though I thought both! I explained that I had been sent for work a workshop hosted in a hotel in Aqaba.

I didn't get the chance to explain that I had been invited to run a workshop for "Creativity for Peace," a wonderful organization I have been honored to work with. Their vision is to be "committed to a time of peace when people and nations coexist by understanding and respecting each other." They focus on "developing the next generation of female leaders and peacemakers in Israel and Palestine."

As I worked with these wonderful, inspiring girls, I saw that their commitment is stronger than the daily discomfort, threat and sometimes even ridicule they face because of their idealism and vision. I was reminded of the power of storytelling and storylistening to transform lives and even society.

Nobody claims that we can change the world with this work, but if we can listen to the story told by 'the enemy' and feel safe in telling our own to them, then perhaps there is hope for a better world. When we tell our story and can listen to theirs, we realise that we are more alike than different; we realise that despite what other people may say and believe Peace is possible.

It was a long journey home. In Dan Yashinsky's amazing book, "Suddenly They Heard Footsteps," he talks about the how the storyteller has been called a Storm Fool - those guys, in Northern Canada, who went from camp to camp telling stories, bringing news, even through the worst storms. Though they were elders and healers, the people thought they were a little mad and so called them 'Storm Fools.' Dan describes their commitment, vision and undying enthusiasm to tell a story with great romance and idealism. This week, as I crossed borders of the land, mind and heart, I was proud to feel that I am following the footsteps of the 'storm fools.'

The ministry official asked me my profession. I said, "Storyteller."

He wrote it down slowly and looked at me with a puzzled expression. I smiled and nodded, and he said, "Wow, nice job!" And I replied, "The best in the world!"

CHAPTER 10 –

Storytelling for developing Outstanding Communication Skills - Preparation

* * *

"Those who do not have power over the story that dominates their lives — the power to retell it, rethink it, deconstruct it, joke about it, and change it as times change — truly are powerless, because they cannot think new thoughts. "

— Salman Rushdie, Novelist

The Story of Star Woman

The Bush People of South Africa believe that there is a race of people who live in the stars. They are a happy and contented people, who want for nothing except for milk. Every so often the Star Women come down to earth, with their unique baskets on their backs, and a bucket in their hand, to take the milk from a farmer's cows. Every Star Woman has her own individual back-basket, which is given to her at birth; it is a beautiful shape, gorgeously coloured and has a tight-fitting lid; in it each Star Woman keeps her most treasured secrets.

One day, a farmer who lived all alone noticed that his milk was disappearing. He would go out in the morning to milk the cows and there would be very little there. When he had discovered this several times, he was determined to find out what was happening. When it got dark, he hid in some bushes at the edge of the field and gazed for hours into the dark. He was getting cold and stiff, and was about to give up, when he heard some sounds far away. It was the sound of women chatting and giggling together, as they got nearer and nearer to the earth. He peered round the bush and saw the group of women with their basket and buckets, and he ran toward them, longing to speak.

When the Star Women saw him, they turned and ran back to their silver threads and started being pulled toward the sky – except for one woman, who tripped and fell, and her silver thread disappeared. The farmer went up to her and asked her to stay with him on his farm, and she agreed on one condition. As long as he promised never to look in her basket, she would come and live with him. She settled down reasonably well; she tended her garden and helped on the farm. Sometimes in the evening she would stand in the doorway and gaze up at the stars, wondering how her family was, and whether she was missed. She felt a little homesick.

After the first few days, the farmer began to get curious about the basket which was standing in the corner or their sitting room. Soon he could contain himself no longer, and when he thought Star Woman was out of the way, he went to look in the basket. Star Woman appeared in the doorway. "But you promised?" she said. The farmer turned and laughed; "But there is nothing there!" he said.

Star Woman turned on her heel and left the house. She reached the gate and looked back one more time. The silver thread was waiting for her, and she went back up to her people in the sky. The issue was not that the farmer had looked in the basket, even though he had promised not to. It was that he could not even see what the basket contained and had laughed as if the basket did not matter.

- Re-told by Sue Jennings PhD., adapted from Lawrence Van der Post "The Heart of the Hunter" and published in Jennings 2005 and 2007 by kind permission.

*A*s we integrate storytelling into coaching practice there are certain skills that make all the difference! You know how you can hear the same joke told by two different people; one is hysterically funny, the other barely makes you smile? Well, the difference is, of course, in the telling. The difference is in the ability to tell a story well.

People often assume that you either can tell a story or you cannot. Somehow, you're just born that way. Well, that may be the case for some people. But for most it's a matter of learning the skills; the skills that you can develop that allow you tell a great story!

In this chapter, we'll discuss some of those crucial skills.

Finding the Story

There are stories everywhere! There are many ways to find stories to tell. There are the obvious sources like books, recordings, and a huge variety of storytelling, or story-related websites and web resources. In addition, there are more and more storytelling festivals and events all over the world – this is certainly the ideal setting to hear great stories!

The other wonderful source for stories is our own experience and by listening carefully to other people as they tell their stories.

When I started out as a storyteller, I would go to meetings and 'tellings,' and there were always brand new storytellers there, frantically taking notes and sometimes even recording the stories being told. I remember being concerned also; where would I find such wonderful stories to tell?

Over the years, I have become more and more aware of the stories around me. A few years ago my coach challenged me to come up with a story every week. I thought that was an impossible assignment (my life is really not that interesting!). Quickly I learned that the stories really are all around me and that if I listen intently, internally and externally, I am rarely caught without a story to tell. There is seldom a situation where a great story does not come to mind!

Story Thematic

Suiting your story to the audience or client is an important skill to acquire.

When you are fully present with your client, you can get a clear understanding of what really matters to them. Only then is it possible to match the story theme with issues that make sense and have meaning for the client.

Here's an example of a client for whom a story seemed a great way to deal with her daughter's recurring nightmares and her subsequent exhaustion!

Mary's 8 year old daughter had become very fearful, and was waking up every night with recurring nightmares. She had been a happy child who particularly loved dancing and playing with her two sisters. She started to express fears that someone would break into their house and that something bad would happen to her father. Mary tried to reassure her, even found a routine where they would check that the doors were locked at night before she went to bed. Nothing helped relieve the nightmares and disruption. In a Story Coaching session, we developed a story process for Mary. We created a story that Mary could tell her daughter; a story about a young girl who loved to dance. The rest of the process is described later. Here is the story–

Once upon a time there was a girl who lived in a small village at the bottom of a hill. She was a happy girl, though she had no brothers or sisters, her mother and father told her that maybe one day she would have them. The girl loved playing outside of their house, in the garden and at the foot of the hill on the edge of the village. She would imagine she was playing hide and seek with her sisters. But her favorite pastime was to dance. She loved dancing. Once a week she went to visit the old woman who lived on the other side of the village who used to be a dancer. She would tell her the stories of her years traveling with a ballet company and dancing all over the country. This little girl thought that this was the most wonderful thing that could ever be…that and having a sister or two!

The old woman told the girl, whose name was Annie, that if she wanted to be a great dancer, she needed to practice and practice and she began to teach her…

After some time she told her that she really needed to get ballet shoes if she was to continue to learn to dance.

Annie came running home that day and told her mother and father that she needed ballet shoes. They decided that her father would have to make a trip to the nearest town to find somewhere to buy ballet shoes. He said he would plan it for the following week.

That night, Annie had a terrible dream. She dreamt that her father went away to the next town, that he bought ballet shoes, but that he got lost and could never find his way home. By the time he got back to the village, she had turned into an old woman and could no longer dance. Annie woke up screaming crying; and nothing her mother or father could say would console her. She was so frightened; and the next day she told her father that he couldn't go away to the town. Her father said, "But Annie, I'm not just going for your ballet shoes. I also have to go for work. I have to go. Don't worry, I'll be fine." Annie was still frightened and though she smiled to her father, she felt so sad inside and was sure that something awful was going to happen.

The next day, Annie woke up and the house was empty. She ran outside and found her mother sitting in a chair on the porch in the sun. She said, "Good morning Annie, I just came outside for some air. I'm not feeling very well..." For the next few days, Annie noticed that her mother seemed very unwell. She was so tired and sick all the time.

When she came home from school her father and mother were waiting for her.

They told her that they both had to make the trip the next day to the neighboring town. Annie would be staying with the old woman she loved, her dance teacher and they would be back the following day. Annie was beside herself with fear and sadness...she felt that something awful might happen. She begged them not to go....

Once she had told this much of the story, Mary stopped. Her daughter asked her what happened next and Mary replied, "I'm not sure, what do you think Annie was scared of? And why? What do YOU think happened next?"

When we discussed the story process, Mary suggested that one way of finishing the story was to make it a happy ending; that the mother is expecting a baby and they come back from the town with a good doctor's report AND the ballet shoes. And then that may continue that Annie learns to be strong and confident, and trust her parents and herself that everything is okay. She can let them go and they will come back; and that she's okay by herself, nothing bad will happen.

The other option we discussed was to simply let her daughter decide how the story would end or at least know that she was the only person who could determine it. This gives her daughter the opportunity to take control of the destiny of the character; it is a clear mirror for the girl taking control of the fears she is experiencing and start to determine her own destiny.

By describing a character that the girl could relate to with specific thematic details that related to her life, Mary helped her daughter work through her fears and come up with coping tactics.

So what happened next?

Well, her daughter asked her to tell her the story several times over the next few days. They discussed how they both felt the story ended, and within a few days, there was clear relief of the nighttime fear symptoms.

In this example, had Mary used a story with an unrelated thematic, her daughter may still have responded well. However, by matching the story theme to elements that her daughter could relate to intimately, the full effect of the story became immediately available to her.

Story Structure

Every story needs a start, middle and end, even if they are not in that order.

In Story Coaching, working with structure can be very useful.

The story structure can be seen as a parallel or metaphor for the main structures that exist in our lives. In the same way that story structure provides the listener with a sense of order and security, life structures have the same role. The difference is that in the story, everything is clear and stated, whereas in life we don't know how it's going to play out. In real life we don't know if the protagonist wins or loses, if they succeed in their mission or fail, if the person lives or dies.

Although this is the wonder and beauty of life, the not knowing, it is also the source of great concern, worry and anxiety; often the very same anxieties and worries that overwhelm our coaching clients.

This is a significant part of the reason that people are so drawn to storytelling, to the comfort of stories. In storytelling, all is defined and definite. It is safe. And whether the end of the story is happy or sad, it is simply known and that provides great comfort.

When we use storytelling, we can play with the structure to allow our listeners wonder and ask themselves questions. We can get our listeners to fill in parts of the story that we leave out. This process allows our listeners to shift perspectives and be creative as to possible outcomes. When we reflect on this in our 'real lives' it becomes a powerful coaching tool. As our clients create the story, or fill in the missing pieces of the story, they understand that they can apply this to their own lives. Once we take responsibility for our life stories, we can change them for the better. This is not about reinventing our history or about somehow 'making up' something new. It is about reframing our stories, telling them from a more positive perspective, one that serves us better. It is an exercise of personal empowerment and realization of life's potential.

Story Interpretation and Intention

Doug Lipman in 'Improving your Storytelling' (August House, 1999) says,

"Although your job… is not usually to impose your interpretation on your listeners, it remains important for you to be clear about that interpretation. If you remain unfocused about the story's primary meaning, the resulting lack of clarity will make your listeners less able to attach their own diverse meanings to the story. When a story is told with clear intention, many meanings can flow out of your one meaning… Once you have articulated it for yourself, you may choose to state it boldly in the story or allow it to remain implicit."

It is very important to identify and understand 'the most important thing' about any story that we choose to tell. Doug's 'Most Important Thing' is really our personal, specific interpretation of the story. When we understand our own interpretation of a story we can make decisions as to how to use the story in our coaching. This intentionality is critical to the effectiveness of the telling and to our ability to be skillful in our Story Coaching.

Often when we hear or read a story that we like, we simply retell it. This happens without reflection, without really understanding what it is about the story that we are attracted to. When we take the time to understand our interpretation and our intention in the telling, then it becomes much more meaningful for us as tellers and for our audience and clients.

The interpretation and intention in Storytelling also serve as a metaphor for helping us discover the same in our lives. Often we go through our day to day without understanding or realizing any sense of intention. It is sometimes a way that we distance ourselves from our values. Using the story analogy, we can start to work with our clients on uncovering and recognizing their values. It is about learning how to live with a whole different level of intention in our lives!

TRY THIS!

(Exercise)

Think about the last story you told, it can be part of a conversation, a written exercise or a story you told in your head.

What was your interpretation of the events of this story?

What was your intention in the telling?

Write this down every time you find yourself telling a story. Common themes may immerge.

Excerpt from a Story Coach's Journal

I'd like to tell you a story. It's about a particular woman, it's about every person. It's about me and it's about you. It is a story about our stories.

It was the first time that the thought arrived clearly and honestly. She wanted to die.

It surprised her at first. And then she remembered her friend who had described the very same thought, the very same feeling.

It was not a random act of hysteria or a long-drawn realization. It was not conclusive. It was simply the thought, almost without any emotion, that if she were to die right now, everything would be so much easier.

Almost immediately she heard her own voice of reason telling her, "Don't be ridiculous. Don't run away. Think of who would suffer." And she recognized the truth of this voice.

She also had a strange, confident calm that made her instinctively understand that she would not DO anything. She would not take any action on the thought.

She simply stood aside from herself and viewed this woman, middle aged, successful, with all the trappings of a joyful life… feeling like she wanted to die.

There are many versions of this story.

Here's one:

She drove her car to the beach. It was a beautiful calm day, the sun was shining; there was a perfect breeze. She carefully parked her car behind the sand dunes and left the keys in the dashboard. She did not think about what she was going to do, she had no sense of purpose or intention. She walked across the sand dunes, arrived at the beach, threw off her shoes and felt the sand gently caress her toes. It was warm on the surface, cooler underneath and as she got closer to the water she felt the dampness seep into her feet. She did not stop at the edge, she just kept on walking. The water was warm and as it lapped gently against her thighs she felt relief. She continued to walk and as the water reached her breasts, the tune that had been in her head escaped her lips. She took a deep breath and smiled as the water went over her head.

Or perhaps it went like this...

She drove to her local coffee shop. The owner greeted her and made her the most perfect cup of coffee, exactly as she likes it. She sat in the corner seat beside the window that looked out onto the street. She leaned her head in her hands and tears started falling down her face, onto the table and into her cup.

She noticed a young child with chocolate all over his face, diving into his brownie. She started to smile and then a little laugh escaped. As the laugh floated up into the warm, moist coffee-house air, it became an idea. She noticed the idea and was startled, "Why have I never thought of this before?"

And for the first time in years, she felt a flutter of excitement deep in her belly. She could really do this. She knew exactly who she needed to tell first. She knew who would help her. She closed her eyes. The tear-stinging eased and she began to imagine her new story. She saw what she was about to create.

Are you wondering what really happened? Here's the thing, it's for you to decide.

Every day we create our life story. Every day we make decisions and choices; and not just about our actions, but also about the way we tell our story.

Our day to day activities are often overwhelming. We are inundated with conflicts, decisions and uncertainty. Most people experience stress as a daily, almost unnoticed, reality. Our stories often contribute to this.

We tell our story of today, yesterday and tomorrow all the time. The narrative choices we make create our reality. And they are choices. That means you can choose something better, a story that serves you well, a reality that allows you to thrive.

So how do we create these empowering, life-giving, abundant stories? Well why not start with a smile; then a little laugh. Let it fly out of your mind and heart and follow it. Watch how it turns into an idea. Then reclaim that smile-idea and take the chance that it might even work!

And then share it; share it with the people you love.

Years ago I wrote a poem about my grandmother and I shared it with my teacher. I was very nervous to show it to him, but when he gave it back to me he wrote these simple words, "Show it to the world."

Now is the time, tell your story, show it to the world!

CHAPTER 11 –

Storytelling for developing Outstanding Communication Skills - Performance

* * *

"We are our stories. We compress years of experience, view and emotion into a few compact narratives that we convey to others and tell to ourselves. That has always been true. But personal narrative has become more prevalent, and perhaps more urgent, in a time of abundance, when many of us are freer to study a deeper understanding of ourselves and our purpose".

- *Dan Pink*, <u>A Whole New Mind</u>

Love is Blind

Once upon a time, before the creation of man, God gathered all the human feelings and qualities, all the virtues and vices into a certain place on earth, and told them to wait for the creation of man.

Time passed and when Boredom had yawned the third time, Madness as mad as always proposed to them; let's play something, let's play hide and seek. Curiosity, unable to hold back asked; "Hide and seek? What is it? Is it a game?" So, Madness explained; "It is easy, I will count to one million, while you other ones hide, and when I'll have finished counting, the first one I have found will take my place and the game goes on." "Wonderful!" shouted Enthusiasm, Euphoria and Excitement, they were so happy that even Doubt was persuaded. But not everyone wanted to take part; Truth preferred not to hide "Why should I, when in the long run I'll be found out?" and Arrogance judged it to be a "very childish and silly game"(but what really disturbed her, was that it was not her idea). So they started the game; One two, three ...Madness began to count.

Tenderness hung on the horn of the moon, Lie said he would hide at the bottom of the lake but he lied and hid behind the rainbow. Faith rose to heaven and Envy hid in the shadow of Triumph who, by his own forces reached the crown of the highest tree. Generosity nearly didn't manage to hide for each place she found seemed more suitable for one of her friends. A crystal lake - the ideal place for beauty! Perhaps a crack in a tree? A perfect place for Shyness! And a gust of wind? A magnificent place for Liberty! Finally she hid in a sunray. Egotism, on the other hand, found right at the beginning a very convenient place, good ventilation, cozy, but only for himself! And Passion and Desire hide in the center of a volcano.

When Madness reached 999,999, Love had not yet found a place to hide. This should be no surprise for we all know how difficult it is to hide love! She was so preoccupied...until she saw a beautiful rose bush and deeply touched she hid between the blossoms. "One Million," Madness shouted, "I'm coming, I'm coming" and as he turned the first one he saw was Laziness, thrown to his feet because he didn't have any energy to hide. Then he found Doubt who was sitting on a fence, unable to decide where to hide. After that Faith was heard discussing theology with God, and Passion and Desire were found because they made the volcano erupt. So he found them all; Fear in a dark cave, and Lie was behind the rainbow (still lying that he was really at the bottom of a lake). Only Love couldn't be found in any place. Madness searched for her everywhere but couldn't find her. And when he was about to give up, when Desperation said that he will never find love, Envy who was envious of Love whispered to Madness: "Love is hiding in the rose bush." Madness saw the rose bush and the blossom...he took a wooden pitch fork, and stabbed at the rose bush, and stabbed and stabbed, till a heartbreaking shout made him stop. And after the shout Love came out covering her face with her hands, from between her fingers, out of her eyes ran two threads of blood, red as the roses. Madness anxious to find Love had taken out Love's eyes with the pitchfork. "What have I done? What have I done?" Madness shouted, "How can I repair it?" he cried and begged for her forgiveness. Hearing the commotion God came back to that place and saw what had happened. "How can I repair it?" asked Madness.

And God answered "You cannot restore her eyes but you can stay with her as her guide."

And so it came about that from that day on, Love is blind and always accompanied by Madness.

Source unknown

*A*n important part of the 'how' of storytelling is the performance. In this chapter we will discuss the storytelling skills that relate to effective delivery of our stories.

Traditionally, the most effective way to tell stories was in person, face-to-face. Nowadays, storytelling occurs through many mediums. It can be incredibly effective when it is used through distance learning or virtual communication.

It is becoming more and more common to coach through virtual means; telephone, teleseminar and webinars. When you coach by phone, you may not have all the physical resources you would have in person, but there are many other advantages. These include minimizing distraction, being super-focused and the time effectiveness of virtual meetings. The very same applies with Story Coaching; it is powerful both virtually and face-to face.

If you want to tell your story effectively, you need to develop expertise in the elements relating to the 'performance' of your story. These 'elements' are relevant depending on the language types you use in the telling, which is determined by the means through which you tell.

For example, if you are telling your story in a teleseminar, clearly you don't need to worry about eye contact. However, this is a crucial element of the successful delivery of a story in person.

First, let's consider the types of Language that we use.

Verbal and Non-verbal language

There has been a lot of research that shows that successful communication is only partially related to the words that a person uses, the material they deliver. A much higher attribution is given to body language and vocal affects.

So, though it is important that the words are meaningful and relevant, that we choose to tell the right stories; how we deliver them is really the most important thing. If we want to have ultimate affect on our listeners and clients, we need to be animated, interesting and engaging. Above all, we need to be authentic.

Body Language

There are five most important elements to body language when we communicate and therefore, when we tell a story (again, keep in mind that these are only relevant depending on the communication mode we use, i.e. Face-to-face or telephone coaching) –

- **Eye Contact** – keeping eye contact with our audience establishes rapport and also gives the added benefit of imparting a sense of credibility. When we really look at our listeners, they believe that we believe what we are telling.

- **Facial Expression** – the expression on our face as we tell a story, tells the audience how we feel and also allows us take on another role in our story. A character can be expressed through our facial expression and the audience gets it straight away. Facial expression can be sensed on the telephone. Try taking to someone on the phone with a smile on your face; see how it affects the call!

- **Posture** – your posture communicates how you feel physically and mentally, how interested you are in your audience and how committed you are to what you are saying. How you hold yourself physically clearly describes your level of confidence in what you are saying, how well you know the story you are telling and how comfortable you are in telling it. We can also sense posture on the phone. Try making a call while you are slumped in your chair or lying down. Then try a similar call while you stand up. The energy levels in your body communicate to your voice and the effect is instantaneous and astounding!

- **Gestures and Movement** – used in storytelling, gestures emphasize key issues in the story, or dramatize events or characters as we tell the story about them. Similar to posture, appropriate movement and gestures can help your energy levels as you speak your story (even if you are on the phone!).

- **Voice – Vocal Effects**

Your voice in Storytelling and Coaching are critical in so many ways – to establish rapport, build confidence and trust, simply be heard, and penetrate to deeper levels of listening in your client.

Your voice tells a lot about you, not just the message you are saying. Think about the voices of the people around you; are they gentle or harsh, loud or soft, varying or mono-tone, irritating or soothing. Do they say 'eh' or 'um,' 'like' or 'you know' a lot? Do they sound smart? Think about the judgments we make based on the voices we hear.

<u>Volume</u> – your voice should be loud enough to be heard, yet not too loud that it is uncomfortable.

<u>Rate</u> - when you vary the pace at which you speak, you project a huge amount of energy and focus during your storytelling. It can also create a wonderful dramatic effect.

<u>Diction</u> – being aware of diction refers to your articulation or pronunciation in speech and the presence of good diction gives a certain impression when a person speaks.

<u>Inflection</u> – by changing the level of your voice within your language, you can add interest to your story. It assumes a certain focus on parts of your language so that you can draw attention to phrases or words.

Seeing the Story

Being able to see the story is a critical part of the successful performance of a story.

A storyteller once told me, "When you see the story, the audience sees the story."

It may sound strange, but it's simply true.

Let me tell you, I am not a very observant person. I can often have a whole conversation with someone and not notice the color of the shirt they are wearing. Yet when I tell a story, I always get the feedback that my stories are very visual, that my listeners can see the story very clearly.

It is not because of my descriptions, I don't give many. It's because I really live in the story, I see it, I feel it; I am present in the story. This causes my audience to experience the feeling that they 'can really see it'!

When I tell the story, I see it in front of me. It lives in a specific space. The king's palace is over the hills to the left; the village is just there beside the forest in front of me and the dragon flies in from the right.   When we have that spatial awareness, when we know where the story lives, it really comes alive for our audience.

Another element of spatial awareness is explained beautifully by Doug Lipman's, "Improving Your Storytelling." Doug talks about 'Orientation in Space.' He says, *"One of the most concrete elements of oral language is the storyteller's spatial relationship to the listeners. Our position relative to our listeners conveys meaning about our relationship and intentions."*

This relates to what I call the *Magic Triangle* between the Story, the Storyteller and the Listener (audience). None of these three elements exists alone, they are all interdependent and I see it as a moving, fluid triangle where each element affects the next. Our spatial choices affect the triangle and ultimately the successful performance of our story.

Audience Assessment

It is very important to prepare thoroughly and get to know your audience. You should find out as much as you possibly can before you go to tell a story (or start a group coaching session). You need to know as much as you can about each individual, their role in the group, their level of influence and their specific needs. You should know as much about the individual and group's attitudes, values, concerns and needs.

Ideally you should find out about any political issues, prior experience and possible predispositions to what you are about to do. You should find out if there are hidden agendas or other political considerations.   If you can anticipate any objections or conflicts in the audience, you are better equipped to deal with them. Similarly, if there are previous positive related experiences, then it can be of great help to you in building rapport and confidence.

Storytelling Environment

Make sure that you check out where you will be before you start your storytelling or story coaching session. Check out the room, the space, and the way the tables or chairs are laid out. If you have any props or equipment you need to get them set up prior to the people arriving. You need a few moments to get comfortable with the space you have before you need to start.

Make sure you factor in this time; always arrive at least 30 minutes before show time!

I always walk the space, I get there in plenty of time, walk around the room, sit in a few of the chairs spread around the room to get a sense of the audience's/client's experience and to feel at home in the space. It relaxes me into the session, physically and emotionally!

Try This!

(Exercise)

What is your biggest challenge in the delivery of your story/presentation?

What is your greatest strength?

Create a check list for the preparation methods that work for you.

Excerpt from a Story Coach's Journal

In the moments before the room filled the thought flashed through my mind. It was the expression of doubt, lack of confidence and failure. It had a tangible emotional and physical effect in that moment.

"So, what's the difference between what you felt then and the people who don't believe in themselves at all?" he asked.

"Well," I answered, "It depends on what wins in terms of your feelings, thoughts and actions, what is the driving force? Is it the thoughts connected to doubt and failure, or do you get rid of those debilitating thoughts and strengthen your beliefs and let that positive force lead you? Do you chose to empower yourself with self-belief and confidence or give in to doubt?"

My partner was in the room. He could feel the tension and nervousness, he sensed that I went into myself for that preparation time and did something that made a difference.

As the room filled beyond capacity, what emerged was, in his words, a transformation. I was confident, comfortable and calm. He said, "Suddenly you created something new, you brought your subject to life, you were inspiring and the people in the room seemed to be quenching a great thirst as they soaked up the knowledge you provided."

So what exactly happened in those precious moments?

Well, firstly, what was the thought? I can tell you that it was very simple, it always is. It goes something like this –

"Who wants to hear a silly story?"

or…

"Are you kidding yourself? These guys are too sophisticated (or experienced, or educated or rich… you can choose!)"

or…

"Why would they want to listen to me?"
or...
"Who am I to think that I can teach them something?"
or...
"Is the material really as good as I think?"
or...
"Will I forget my stuff?"

You see there is no end of self-sabotaging stories that we tell ourselves. The question is how do we get rid of them, what can we do to make ourselves strong, confident and really shine?

There are four areas that you need to cover; physical, intellectual, spiritual and emotional.

Your physical preparation should be to acknowledge your nervousness for the positive effect that it has on you. The rush of adrenalin gives you wonderful energy that you can channel into a positive force for your work. Also, you can recite some tongue twisters and pull funny faces so you stretch and warm up your facial muscles and voice. You can jump a few times or take a fast walk, or pat down your body (cup both hands and work up from your feet to you head); choose what feels right for you so that you get this positive energy flowing through your body.

Your intellectual preparation involves simply knowing your stuff! You need to practice, practice, practice and then when you're sure you know your material perfectly, you need to practice some more!

Your spiritual preparation involves connecting to that higher place (whatever you choose to call it!) and acknowledge this presence in your life, in the room and within you. Once you feel connected, you can enjoy the sense of blessing and abundance within you, and your ability to share that with your audience.

And finally your emotional preparation; I recommend a mantra. For me, it's simple. "Trust the stories, trust the process, trust." I repeat this in my head in the last few moments before I start, and it gets me right where I need to be.

Part of my emotional preparation for this specific event was in knowing that my partner was in the room and witnessing this transformation. It got me thinking how often the people we choose to spend our lives with, our partners, family and best friends, never actually get to see us in this moment of great passion, focus and clarity doing what clearly we were always meant to do.

What happens when they see the transformation, when they witness you at your best, radiating the joy of whatever it is that makes you shine?

When there is this quiet, appreciative support, it's almost like a shadow in the room; an angel that protects and guides you with love, seeing you as your true higher self. It is a blessing.

Have you ever shared that amazing moment with someone meaningful in your life?

What is your practice that gets you performing at your best?

CHAPTER 12 –

Storytelling for Outstanding Coaching Skills

* * *

"Storytelling is a healing art that can draw out the innate wisdom within us."

—Nancy Mellon in "Body Eloquence"

Maria Guadalupe

She lived in New York, with her mother in an apartment in the middle of town. Maria wasn't particularly tall and she wasn't particularly small. She wasn't particularly beautiful or particularly ugly. She wasn't particularly dark or light. She wasn't particularly anything, she was simply average.

She had a pretty good job, not particularly interesting or too boring a job. She went to that job every day for four and a half years when this particular day came about.

Maria this morning, like every morning, left her apartment building and began walking the four blocks to her office. At the end of the block where she lived, she noticed a new shop, it was a hat shop.

Maria was never interested in hats before but for some reason she felt drawn to the shop. She went inside and began to look around. Inside the shop, there was just one customer, a woman with her young daughter. She was trying on some hats with the shop-keeper helping her. Maria walked around, looking here and there. Then she looked up to the third shelf where there was a hat that drew her attention. She reached up, took it down and put in on her head.

Then she looked in the mirror and for the first time, in as long as Maria could remember, she saw a reflection of herself and actually liked what she saw. Not only that, but as she looked in the mirror, the young girl, the daughter of the other shopper, leaned over and said, "Mommy, Mommy look at that lady, she's put on that lovely hat, doesn't she look beautiful?" The mother turned around and said to Maria, "That hat really does suit you! Wow, you look wonderful!"

Maria was delighted, she couldn't remember a time when she had liked how she looked and no one had ever told her that she looked beautiful before. She immediately decided to buy the hat. She walked over to the counter, paid for the hat and walked out onto the street.

Maria walked on to work but now she could hear the sounds of the birds tweeting and she noticed that the sun was shining and there was a nice cool breeze. She just felt wonderful. As she got to the corner of the next block there was a young man sitting at a café. He looked over, smiled at her and asked if she would like to join him for coffee. She smiled, laughed and walked on. A few blocks later she arrived at her office.

The doorman opened the door and she walked inside. He said to her, "Good morning, how are you today?" It was the first time anybody had ever said good morning to Maria as she walked into her office building. She went towards the elevators and as she got there someone, inside the elevator, put their hand out and stopped the door closing so that she could get in. This kind of thing never ever happened to Maria.

She went up to her office and as she walked in the secretary at the main entrance said, "Maria you look great, how are you?" Inside her office people really noticed her, her boss came over, chatted with her and even began to flirt with her. He invited her out for lunch!

Maria had a wonderful, wonderful day and the end of this magical day she stepped out of the elevator and decided that today she would treat herself to a cab ride home. As soon as she put her hand out, two cabs stopped right in front of her, the doors flew open and she got inside one and was driven home. She had had the most amazing day!

She arrived home, walked upstairs and went to her apartment. She put the key in the lock, opened the door and her mother stood on the other side and said, "Maria, wow you look amazing, what's happened to you today?"

Maria laughed and said, "Oh mum, it's just because of this silly hat." Her mother said, "What silly hat?" Maria put her hand to her head and realized that there was no hat there. She thought, what did I do with it? Where did I leave it? Did I leave it in the taxi? No. Did I leave it at my desk? No. Did I leave it in the restaurant where I went for lunch? No. She thought back through the day and tried to remember where she could possibly have left her hat. Did she leave it in the office somewhere else? No.

Then she remembered, that morning when she had gone into the hat shop, she tried on the hat and then went to pay for it. There she took it off and placed it on the counter. She took the money out, paid and walked out of the shop, without the hat.

Source Unknown

Recently I had the opportunity to spend some time with a few of my dear Storytelling colleagues, a wonderful group of inspired, talented people who share my passion to tell stories. We were discussing the transformation of the story as it moves from written form to the oral tale. What happens when we tell the story that we have just read? Or that someone has just told us? How does the story change?

Part of the discussion reminded me of that game we used to play as kids 'Chinese Whispers'- where someone would whisper a message to someone else and it would be passed down the line. The end result was a completely distorted and usually very funny message.

You see, the truth is that when I tell a story, I tell "My Story."

Even if I'm telling the story of "Little Red Riding Hood," it's my version. The way I remember it told to me as a child, or the book that I read later and then all kinds of other influences. In truth, the way I choose to tell a story will include my attitudes and my beliefs. My personality and my values all come through in the story.

When I tell a story, I tell my story.

I tell who I am, or at least, how I see myself. If I feel strong and positive, it's in my story. If I feel hurt or misjudged, it's in my story. If I feel like a success or a failure, it's in my story. If I feel victorious or like a victim, it's in my story.

If we pause for a moment and think about how we tell our stories, and of course why we tell them, we can begin to tell more empowering stories, stories of fun and laughter, stories that lead us to a more positive experience of our own lives. It really is that simple. When we tell stories that are amusing and stories that are uplifting, we really can make our lives more fun and more joyful. When we tell stories of resilience and strength, we really do feel stronger.

The act of storytelling is itself a powerful coaching moment.

There are specific Coaching tools that can be derived directly from Storytelling; we will discuss some of these tools in this chapter.

Coaching Model - The Story Journey

This Model looks at the Coaching Journey through the eyes of a storyteller. As we experience our lives, we tell our story. The narrative that we choose to tell defines our experience.

The terms Protasis, Epitasis and Catastrophe are the 3 acts of the Classical Greek narrative structure. They form the basic structure for all storytelling.

Examining the classic narrative structure, we can apply coaching activities to the stages of the journey. This way we see how the story maps onto our best (coaching) practice.

Protasis (Exposition, Set Up)

- *active, attentive listening to the client's narrative*

- *validation & acknowledgement*

- *goal searching*

Epitasis (Confrontation)

- *challenging questions*

- *goal setting*

- *changing perspective, reframing*

- *visualization*

Catastrophe (Resolution)

- *empowerment*

- *celebration*

In each of these stages the coaching process is empowered by using this narrative approach, the Story Coaching Methodology maps directly to classical storytelling!

Using Storytelling as a guide, a metaphor, an illustrative tool and a resource of age-old wisdom, we achieve greater success and demonstrate excellence in our Coaching Skills.

Values

I don't know about you, but I hate the traditional values exercises. You know the one – it goes something like this:

You're given a list of 50 values and asked to choose the 15 most important values, in your opinion. Once you have that you're asked to get rid of 5 that you have chosen, then another 5. The 5 that are left, you then have to prioritize.

The problem is that it's really difficult. I always think, but I want them all! I don't want to have to choose between health and wealth, or family and freedom. It's so confusing!

In Story Coaching, we have a different way of achieving the very same result. You ask your client to simply tell a story. It doesn't really matter what story, it could be a fairy tale or a personal story, or it may be the story of what they would like to create. If you listen closely, you will hear their values. You can write them down and I promise, by the time they have finished telling their story, you will have their top 5 values. Try it!

Goal Setting

Similarly with goal setting, you can place it in narrative context and the task becomes simple and empowering.

All you need to ask is "Tell me the story of how your life will look?" and encourage them to go into details. Through the story process, discovering it and telling it, your clients' goals become crystal clear.

There are other questions you can ask to help your client become clear on her/his goals:

- Let's work into your story how you will take new actions, how you will continue to find new opportunities.

- How will you learn more? Now, retell your story.

- What other ideas can you incorporate in your new story?

- What are other solutions?

- Well done, I love your story! But keep going I want another version! A bigger and better one now!

Throughout the coaching process, the client is retelling the goal setting story and what unfolds is the story of success!

Acknowledgement & Recognition

A film that I really love is called, "Shall We Dance" with Richard Gere and Susan Sarandon. There's this great scene where the wife, Mrs. Clark (Sarandon) is in a bar talking to the Private Detective she has hired because she suspects her husband (Gere) is having an affair. She asks, "What is the purpose of marriage?" And then answers, "We need a witness to our lives….you promise (in marriage) to care about everything…" She continues, "Your life will not go unnoticed, your life will not go un-witnessed."

This is so relevant for coaching, particularly Story Coaching. When we allow the space for our clients to tell their story, to finally be heard, we acknowledge and recognize them. They no longer go unnoticed, their challenges and triumphs are no long un-witnessed.

This is one of the powerful outcomes of the Story Coaching process.

Sometimes just telling your story is a healing in itself.

"Look at her hands," he said.

"Look at how the beauty of the whole dance is expressed in her hands."

The twisting, flying graceful movements of the flamenco dancer's hands were, indeed, exquisite.

My gracious neighbor at the dinner table explained where the traditional dance came from and told me how it was part of his upbringing in the south of Spain.

But what drew me in so intensely was the passion.

The pillars and dome of the grand hall were draped in colored light with dramatic effect. The windows were long and wide, overlooking the spectacular architecture of the surrounding buildings, each one signifying a different era of the history of this simply beautiful Spanish city.

The eyes of the dancers and the expression on their faces told the story that was mirrored in their movements. I imagined the longing, the estrangement and the reuniting of hearts, bodies and souls. I was intrigued and delighted, delirious and heartbroken all at the same time in the magical space of the dance.

It was astounding, it was gorgeous!

Coffee was served in tiny cups, hot and strong, with leaf-like slivers of chocolate. The conversations around the table danced between the delicious food, wonderful music and spectacular entertainment.

"So what IS your story?" I asked. He blushed, looked down at the table and his eyes danced. "Oh, I'm sorry," I said, "I don't mean to pry."

"It's okay," he replied, "It's just I haven't really told that story before."

And then he gave me the gift of his story; a story of duty, sadness, madness, loss and enormous love. I took his hand and thanked him.

After we finished the meal, we all ascended the grand, regal staircase to the floor above where music and dancing awaited us. And we danced until the early hours, weaving in and out of strangers held together by the throb of music and intimacy of the moment.

The next day, when we said our goodbyes, my dining friend came up to me and took my hand. "Thank you," he said, "thank you for asking me to tell you my story. It has made all the difference."

His eyes were shy but his voice strong. He nodded, smiled and walked away.

When you tell your story you discover who you are.

Telling your story helps you heal, simply by the telling. And it connects you deeply with your listener.

Every time I have been blessed by the gift of someone's story, a part of it lives in me forever.

I see that we are all collectors of these magnificent stories of the human condition. We experience our stories and the stories of others as an emotional, physical intimacy.

It is powerful beyond measure.

Action Planning

Your story is your vision. As you work with your clients to articulate their vision, to tell the story of what they want to achieve, then you can develop and maintain the coaching plan for continuity in the process.

Identify SMART goals and chart a success line, noting all successes along the way. One way to do this is to have your client create, tell and record their success stories. The very telling of these success stories attracts more of the same!

Creating Awareness

Using Storytelling in your Coaching Practice enhances your skills as a Coach. There are many ways that this expertise comes to light, always focusing on what value you can offer your client in accompanying them on their own personal hero's journey.

Here are some of the highlights of the Story Coaching Methodology:

- Stories assist in the integration of all kinds of information from many different stories. Often it's the story that helps it all come together in an appropriate and attainable manner.

- Listening to stories and learning to tell our own stories works as a tool for inquiry, helping our clients attain greater clarity, understanding and awareness

- Using storytelling to shift perspectives, we uncover underlying concerns and determine the difference between fact and interpretation.

- Stories, both heard and told, help our clients discover new ideas to assist in moving into action and initiate real change.

- The stories that our clients tell help them identify their own strengths and areas for growth and learning

- Using stories we can assist our clients in distinguishing between the trivial and significant both in issues and behaviors; they learn to recognize their own behavioral patterns.

Managing Progress & Accountability

Similar to the way in which we set goals and create a success story log, this is also the way to manage progress in the Story Coaching process.

The client's story has sub-stories along the way; these stories need to be told. Each session and sub-story may require action, as a Story Coach you will suggest action and keep your client accountable.

As you follow your plan, using the Coaching model, you can monitor the client's story as she/he tells it again and again throughout the process. It is this telling and retelling of the story that helps the Story Coach track and reflect the client's progress in the process.

The 'No-Story' Space

For many years I have been aware of the work of Byron Katie. I have always sensed that it is deeply connected to the Story

Coaching work, but I was not sure of the nature of this connection until relatively recently.

I decided to take a course for practitioners of "The Work." I loved the program and found that doing "The Work" on a daily basis is simply magical! And finally, I discovered the connection.

There are times when our stories do us a great disservice, our stories sabotage us; they cause us great pain and suffering. These are the stories that leave us stuck, unhappy, desperate and with a sense that we are unable to change. We need a tool, a resource that can help us understand, accept and be at peace with these stories. We need to get to the bottom of these debilitating stories that we have created and do us no good.

"The Work" of Byron Katie is the perfect tool to do this. With her simple and enormously powerful 4 questions and turnarounds, we can breakdown these stories and get beyond the pain and suffering that they cause us.

For more on "The Work," please read Byron Katie's "Loving What Is." Here you will see how reality is always much kinder than the stories we create about it and how little we tend to stay in our own business!

Excerpt from a Story Coach's Journal

THE MIRACLE

I witnessed a miracle this week. I know I'm being a little dramatic, but it really seemed like there was magic in the air. Some people would say that it wasn't anything special, a pretty normal event that was bound to happen sometime, but I think it was a miracle! The truth is I've started to notice miracles in the most unexpected places.

My second son is 8, as I write this I hear him correcting me, 8 and a half! He's a smart kid, very energetic and a real dreamer. At times he gets so immersed in the world he has dreamed up around him that he doesn't see or hear anything else. He loves stories and puzzles, and especially numbers. Though he loves to be active he's not very graceful, in fact he was even diagnosed (yes, literally diagnosed) once as 'clumsy.'

He has always avoided learning to ride his handed down bicycle.

This is a kid who often talks about being scared. We talk about how everyone has fears but he thinks he has more than everyone else. Even still, his fears don't stop him from doing anything that the other kids do. He just tells me later that it was scary.

But not when it comes to cycling, he just won't even try it because he says he can't.

Then this week he simply said, "Let's go and ride the bikes." He got out on the street with a determined expression and set off. He started to ride his bike! It was a miracle!

I don't know why suddenly this week he knew he could do it. All I know is that when he circled around and came back to me, he had a red face, a grin from ear to ear and a new sparkle in his eye. "I did it, and it's so fun, and it's easy, not scary at all!"

How many times do we hesitate and stop ourselves from trying something new because it seems scary? You know what it's like. You want a change, a new job or to follow your dream and start a new business. Then you get busy listening to the internal and external voices that tell you all the reasons why you'd be taking a risk that is too big; or about all the hundreds of other people that have tried and failed. You start listing all the reasons that this idea is scary and impossible; instead of listing all the reasons why you were born to do this and are bound to succeed. Go on, dare to try something new!

How often are we willing to put our fears aside and do something just because it looks like fun?

You remember how when you were a kid you would go to the fairground and stand in line for the biggest, scariest rides? Nowadays you think that the moment of fun is really not worth all that fear! Have you considered that it actually might be worth it? Try it!

Why do we make choices based on what's known and safe rather than what we really want?

Maybe it's time to leave 'known and safe' tucked away nice and happily in an old closet and start digging out what we really want to do! You'll thank yourself for it and eventually, over time, you'll sort out your stuff and throw out 'known and safe' without even noticing!

Can you imagine that grin from ear to ear and the new, brave sparkle in your eyes?

Look in the mirror – make it happen - start noticing and you may even witness a miracle!

CHAPTER 13 –

Story Coaching, What next? The story continues...

* * *

"We live in story like a fish lives in water. We swim through words and images siphoning story through our minds the way a fish siphons water through its gills. We cannot think without language, we cannot process experience without story."

— *Christina Baldwin, Author, "StoryCatcher: Making Sense of our Lives Through the Power and Practice of Story"*

S torytelling is a powerful force in humanity and in the world, there is no doubt. Storytelling is a powerful tool in coaching, and Story Coaching is the way to go about harnessing this tool and maximizing its effects as we work with our clients.

Using Story to talk about your business is the way to go about getting clients. Your story is not just an added irrelevant detail that is disconnected from your business. Your story is who you are in the world AND in your business.

When you discover your story and start using it in your business, you will become clear about who you need to be working with and what work you need to be doing.

Your story is the key to understanding where you can perform best and what services you need to be offering. Your story is the key to understanding how to create meaningful and profitable activity in your business.

Recently I was at an excellent event for entrepreneurs where the astoundingly brilliant lecturer said something that really surprised me.

He said, "You need to uncover your story by speaking about your greatest struggles and pain from a place of empowerment."

He's absolutely right, but that is SO DIFFICULT! For so many people, just thinking about their pain and greatest struggles in life is completely overwhelming. Why would they want to tell the story of it? How could you bear to?

Well, Story Coaching is the answer. It is the way to understand stories, create and recreate stories and reinvent yourself as an entrepreneur in your coaching.

Let me tell you a story....

While the incredible summer weather persisted, we took advantage of it and went to the beach. The kids were excited to be taking out the kayak and were bickering about who would go first! The sea was calm and cool and there was a soft breeze sweeping in across the beach. The boys immediately ran into the water and yelped with delight!

I have always loved the ocean. I feel at home there and it brings me back to my childhood where I spent so many days at the beach. The sea in Ireland is much colder and rougher but that's not to say that the hidden currents here are any safer. As kids we always had rules about respecting the power of the ocean and staying safe. I'm very firm about this with my kids too. They get so excited by being in the water and feel so safe there that sometimes they forget to stay in the shallower area. I make sure not to take my eyes off them!

It was my turn for the kayak. I love paddling out far from the beach where I feel the wind stronger and enjoy the sensation of my arm muscles stretching more and more with each stroke. There is a silence out there that is magical and I always feel a sense of calm as I pull away from the beach. My son was on the back and he was being playful. As we got out to the deepest point of our short journey, he started to rock the kayak. "Don't you feel like a swim?" he laughed. I acted shocked at first and tried to counter-balance his rocking. And then the kayak tipped over and we both fell out, laughing and shrieking from the hit of the cold water.

I lifted myself up onto the kayak first and wiggled into place. Then my son tried. He pulled himself up but kept falling off the end. Then he lay over the top but each time he turned over, he pulled us both into the water. After about 6 attempts, he decided to swim to shore.

I paddled slowly after him thinking about what had just happened.

I'm a great fan of rocking the boat. I always want to feel the shock of the cold water and know that I'll always be able to get myself back on board. My son had just learnt the lesson that if you can't get back up, it might not be such a good idea to jump over!

When we reached the shore he leapt back on, grabbed the paddle and headed off but I noticed that he didn't go out quite so far this time.

I swam after him and suggested that he practice getting in and out, when he was out of his depth, to figure out the best way to get back in.

Within a really short time, he was hopping up and down from the kayak to the water and back again with a huge grin on his face. He could now capsize and recover smoothly and quickly and I noticed that he was also paddling much faster now. The confidence he had gained by knowing that he could recover from anything meant that he moved even faster in the water.

When we have enough confidence to know that we can recover from anything, we feel more comfortable taking risks. Your business story is what creates this confidence. When you know your story, it allows you the freedom and self-reliance to take bigger leaps in your business. You may hit some unexpected cold water but your story will keep you afloat!

R eading this book is just the start.
     And by the way, I'm so glad you are here with me on this journey.
You see I have a mission. Yes, I have a dream.

I imagine a time where all Coaches will understand the power of Storytelling to impact their lives and the lives of their clients.

I imagine a time where there will be a network of Story Coaches worldwide bringing this expertise to the forefront of the coaching industry.

Will you join us? Will you reinvent yourself?

35 years ago, I revealed a terrible secret.

I told my friend something that she was not supposed to know. It was a dreadful secret that had been held in their family forever.

She was innocent and the news was devastating. It was information that would affect the rest of her life.

I got into terrible trouble.

I had not thought about this incident for years, perhaps not since it happened, that is until this week.

You see, this week, I did it again.

I revealed a secret to people I care about, it was something they were not supposed to know. And yes, I got into trouble again.

So it got me thinking about secrets. And why it seems that I have such a hard time keeping them!

In both cases, I was also innocent. I did not know that the information was a secret.

Now you'd be right in asking, "What happens when you tell a storyteller a fascinating story, she's not going to tell it?"

In my family, they told the children everything.

At least that's how it felt to us kids. There were no secrets. What was spoken about was discussed amongst us all. Silly me, I thought all families were like that.

It seems that it has taken me 35 years to realize that this is not the case!

It amazes me that, once again, life has gone the full circle, the full story circle. In dealing with my faux-pas this week, I have had the wonderful opportunity to dig up the old story and work through the pain, the injustice of a young child punished for a mistake.

Story work does that. Our stories go round and round, the themes interweaving, the lessons being learned and relearned until we heal.

At first, I felt frustrated and angry. How was I supposed to know? Why don't they say what they want? It's not fair, I was just trying to be friendly and pass on happy information.

But then I remembered my old story. I felt the pain of my 7 year old self, being yelled at and ridiculed because I had told this terrible secret.

I had caused great pain to the adults who had tried to protect their children and the children who did not know. I felt guilty and angry. I was wrong but I didn't know any better, no one told me not to tell.

So now the adult, I went for a walk. I told both of the stories. I did "The Work."*

And the healing began.

Stories are meant to be told and secrets often cause pain. In both of my stories, everyone did their best. We are all innocents.

But the one thing I know is that in all cases, when we tell the story, we begin to heal.

And it doesn't end there. It's not just about healing.

The wonder and beauty of our stories is that as we tell them, we not only heal old wounds, we discover how our struggle is our greatest source of empowerment.

It is the learning that we gain through our healing stories that makes us great. It is the telling of the struggle that lets us soar to greater heights.

Stories are meant to be told.

What stories have you told in order to heal?

What are the stories that empower your greatest self?

Welcome to the world of Story Coaching.

Stephen Denning in "The Springboard" says, "*When we hear a story that touches us profoundly, our lives are suffused with meaning… The connectedness between the self and the universe has been reset. The story is something that comes from outside. But the meaning is something that emerges from within. When a story reaches our hearts with deep meaning, it takes hold of us. Once it does so, we can let it go, and yet it remains with us. We do not weary of this experience. Why should we? Once we have had one story, we are already hungry for another. We want more in case it too can transmit the magic of connectedness between ourselves and the universe."*

Fresh out of coaching school, I had some great life and business experience; I even had pretty significant coaching experience. I had some great skills. I had a really nice office and a good computer. I had a creative business card and the start of a website.

I had no clients.

I had no idea where to get clients.

I had no income.

But I could tell a good story. And that was a great start!

So, why not cut your journey short. Take the road less travelled and make your mark in the world and in the coaching industry. Become a Story Coach and see your business and life move in new, exciting, and creative directions.

Understanding the power of Storytelling and taking the leap into Story Coaching, you will be empowered to be the very best version of yourself, the very best coach. The impact will be profound.

Don't stop here! Find your Story. Find out the ways that Story Coaching can empower your life and your business.

And most importantly, tell your story!

CPSIA information can be obtained at www.ICGtesting.com
Printed in the USA
BVOW06s1818250615

406211BV00013B/322/P